MW01124141

LEARN TO PRAY

Dr. Tom Williams

All Scriptures used in this book are from the King James Bible.

To order more of these books and other materials
by Dr. Williams, please call or write:

Tom Williams' Worldwide Ministries

4000 Brookside Court NE

Lanesville, IN 47136

Phone: 812-952-4245

Fax: 812-952-4246

Website: www.twwm1.com

E-mail: tomwilliams@twwm1.com

Published by Faithful Life Publishers
North Fort Myers, FL 33903

FaithfulLifePublishers.com
888.720.0950

TABLE OF CONTENTS

HOW TO PRAY

INTRODUCTION

Sometimes you wonder why it is that oft times when we pray,
The things we ask the Lord to do don't happen in a day.
But if we look into God's Word, as we should every day,
We find that many had to wait in much the selfsame way.

I'm sure that Moses didn't think, while under God's command,
That it would take him 40 years to reach the Promised Land.
Did Noah think when he laid the keel to start the famous Ark,
That God would hold him all those years, before he would embark?

God said, "Abraham, from thy loins a nation shall arise,
As countless as the ocean, sand, or stars in evening skies."
But many years went swiftly by,
Before a son in error had given to Abraham an answer to his prayer.

And so my friends, great truths we learn, as we pass beneath the rod.
The time to pray is every day and leave the answers to God.

~Selected

THOUGH YOU MAY have to wait on God, you need to continual-ly pray. *"And he spake a parable unto them to this end, that men ought always to pray, and not to faint"* (Luke 18:1). You need to learn that about prayer. Sometimes you may receive answers immediately, while at other times the answers are delayed.

> *"Then said he unto me, Fear not, Daniel: for from the first day that thou didst set thine heart to understand, and to chasten thyself before thy God, thy words were heard, and I am come for thy words. But the prince of the kingdom of Persia withstood me one and twenty days: but, lo, Michael, one of the chief princes, came to help me; and I remained there with the kings of Persia. Now I am come to make thee understand what shall befall thy people in the latter days: for yet the vision is for many days"* (Daniel 10:12-14).

LEARN TO DEVELOP A PRAYER LIFE

The Lord Jesus Christ had a prayer life; the apostle Paul had a prayer life; other saints of God have had a prayer life; and God wants you to have a prayer life. Most people do not pray however, because they do not know how to pray. Christians don't instantly possess a prayer life; they have to develop it over time. Some Christians have a prayer *time*, but few have a prayer *life*. A prayer time is setting aside a specific amount of time in order to meet with God in prayer. A prayer life includes times of closet praying, but it also encompasses praying about every aspect of life throughout the day and night, whether it is praying about something simple or something more complex. The difference between a prayer life and a prayer time is that with a prayer life you literally **pray about everything**. Our Lord Jesus Christ did nothing without prayer because to Him, prayer was a very extension of His life. Like breathing, it was essential and not an option.

Pray for safety in travel. Before driving anywhere, pray that God will keep you safe, then thank Him afterward for safe travels. Never get in the car and leave before asking God for His protection. Pray for both the "small" and "large" needs of your life. Pray for one another. Learn to pray about **everything**!

Developing a prayer life takes time like it does for someone who is learning to run long distances. Learning to pray does not occur overnight; it is learned over a period of time. As God's people, we need to realize this about prayer. There is much to pray for; and if we did what God said and prayed for one another, we would begin to spend more in prayer. Pray over a church list of its members. Pray for the Pastor and his family. Pray for your children and grandchildren. The average Christian parents in America pray two minutes a day for their children. No wonder our homes have failed! We will learn to pray by praying. Some prayer lists you can compile could include:

1) The sick
2) Widows
3) Church members
4) Missionaries

To Whom Do You Pray?

We **do not** pray to the Holy Spirit. When we are asking in prayer for anything, we ask God the Father in the name of Jesus. *"But the Comforter, which is the Holy Ghost, whom the Father will send in my name, He shall teach you all things, and bring all things to your remembrance, whatsoever I have said unto you"* (John 14:26).

The Spirit of God will never say anything that Christ did not teach, and He did not teach us to pray to the Holy Spirit; therefore, you do not pray to the Holy Spirit because the Holy Spirit didn't come to be prayed to.

Neither do we ask Jesus for anything. We cast our cares upon Him—read 1 Peter 5:7 and Psalm 55:22—but according to Scriptures, we are not to petition or ask Him for anything. Therefore, when we pray, we pray to God, our Father. It is to Him that we make our petition. The Lord Jesus taught His disciples to pray, saying, *"Our Father..."* (Matthew 6:9; Luke 11:2).

> *"But thou, when thou prayest, enter into thy closet, and when thou hast shut thy door, pray to thy Father which is in secret; and thy Father which seeth in secret shall reward thee openly... After this manner therefore pray ye: Our Father which art in heaven, Hallowed be thy name"* (Matthew 6:6, 9).

> *"And it came to pass, that, as he was praying in a certain place, when he ceased, one of his disciples said unto him, Lord, teach us to pray, as John also taught his disciples. And he said unto them, When ye pray, say, Our Father which art in heaven, Hallowed be thy name. Thy kingdom come. Thy will be done, as in heaven, so in earth"* (Luke 11:1-2).

PRAYER IS PERSONAL

It is a wonderful truth that we can call God "our Father." Abraham couldn't call Him Father. King David couldn't call Him Father. Moses couldn't call Him Father. None of the great prophets could call God their Father. When they addressed Him, they called Him *Jehovah, El Shaddai,* and other names; but they could not yet call Him Father because Christ had not yet come.

It was the Lord Jesus Christ and His shed blood on Calvary's cross which opened God's throne of grace to us and gave us the privilege to call Him Father. Addressing Almighty God as "our Father" opens to us a greater depth of intimacy with Him. Yes, He is Lord. Yes, He is God. However, when we call Him Father, we are addressing Him in the most personal way possible.

Pray Expecting

Attempt great things for God, expect great things from God.
– William Carey

"And they blessed Rebekah, and said unto her, Thou art our sister, be thou the mother of thousands of millions, and let thy seed possess the gate of those which hate them" (Genesis 24:60).

When we pray, we need to take hold of God's promises and **expect** Him to answer. We expect answers by faith. Believe that He is able! Believe that He has all power! Believe His Word! The Bible says, *"Now unto him that is able to do exceeding abundantly above all that we ask or think, according to the power that worketh in us"* (Ephesians 3:20). Believe it. It is our unbelief that hinders God from working. *"And he did not many mighty works there because of their unbelief"* (Matthew 13:58).

It is not that God is not able; it is that we do not believe. Jesus told the father of the demoniac son, *"If thou canst believe, all things are possible to him that believeth"* (Mark 9:23).

We need to believe the God of the Bible. The God *"who hath gathered the wind in his fists"* (Proverbs 30:4a); the God *"who shut up the sea with doors, when it brake forth, as if it had issued out of the womb… and brake up for it my decreed place; and set bars and doors, and said, Hitherto shalt thou come, but no further: and here shall thy proud waves be stayed"* (Job 38:8, 10-11). He is the God whose *"clouds are the dust of his feet"* (Nahum 1:3).

Almighty God has control of all His creation and of our lives; He desires that we believe Him and expect great things from Him when we pray. We stand on the promises He has made and believe that He— the only One—is able to fulfill them.

LESSON ONE

HOW TO PRAY QUESTIONS

1. Prayer isn't always answered immediately. Give an example from the Bible of someone who had to wait for his or her answer.

_____

_____

2. Name two people in the Bible who had a prayer life.

_____

_____

3. In your own words, explain what "Pray about everything" means.

_____

_____

4. Find a verse that instructs us to pray. Write reference below.

_____

_____

5. Give examples of things in your everyday life that you can pray about.

_____

_____

6. For what purpose was the Holy Spirit sent to us? Give a verse to back up your answer.

_____

_____

7. Is there ever a time that we would ask Jesus for something?

_____

_____

8. For what purpose do we pray to the Heavenly Father?

_____

_____

9. Why is it that you and I can call God "Father" but those in the Old Testament could not?

_____

_____

10. What does addressing God as our Father do?

_____

_____

THE PRIORITY OF PRAYER

INTRODUCTION

MOST PRAYER SERVICES in our churches today have been reduced to being like a small tip at either the start or end of a service. There is very little, if any, *"effectual fervent"* praying (James 5:16) or leading of the Holy Spirit in prayer.

> *"Likewise the Spirit also helpeth our infirmities: for we know not what we should pray for as we ought: but the Spirit itself maketh intercession for us with groanings which cannot be uttered"* (Romans 8:26).

If you look at prayer collectively in our churches, our homes, our Christian schools, our Bible conferences, or anywhere else, you will find that there isn't much prayer taking place. It has been that way down through the centuries; however, God has put a great priority on prayer in His Word. We read about some men and women from the past who were wonderful prayer warriors. We are told, by tradition at least, that the apostle James was called "camel knees" because he spent so much time kneeling in prayer that he had built up large calluses on his knees much like we might see on a camel.

There were men like "praying John Hyde" who labored in prayer so much that revivals occurred frequently. Shortly before his death, he was winning five souls a day to Christ. E. M. Bounds wrote much on prayer and prayed much; and at the end of his life he was noted to have said that he believed he had taught one other man to truly pray. Lillian Trasher, by prayer and faith, built an orphanage in Egypt at a time when there weren't any. God knows you and me and He knows whether or not we pray.

The Christian's vitality is found in prayer to God as we declare our complete dependence upon Him. If we are going to possess this power of God in our Christian living and service, we need to learn from those who have prayed, understand that with God, prayer is a priority, and begin to pray. If you would do a search through your Bible with some helpful Bible tools you will find that the words *pray, prayeth, praying,* and *prayer* are mentioned more than 500 times. The words p*reacheth, preaching,* and *preach* are mentioned less than 200 times. Prayer is mentioned three times as many as preaching; therefore, it is apparent that God does not major on preaching; He majors on praying. It is praying that is going to affect the preaching and be mightily used to turn hearts toward God. The greatest example of prayer, of course, is the prayer life of our Lord Jesus Christ.

GOD PUTS A PRIORITY ON PRAYER

"Thus saith the LORD, Keep ye judgment, and do justice: for my salvation is near to come, and my righteousness to be revealed. Blessed is the man that doeth this, and the son of man that layeth hold on it; that keepeth the sabbath from polluting it, and keepeth his hand from doing any evil. Neither let the son of the stranger, that hath joined himself to the LORD, speak, saying, The LORD hath utterly separated me from his people: neither let the eunuch say, Behold, I am a dry tree. For thus saith the LORD unto the eunuchs that keep my sabbaths, and choose the things that please me, and take hold of my covenant; Even unto them will

I give in mine house and within my walls a place and a name better than of sons and of daughters: I will give them an everlasting name, that shall not be cut off. Also the sons of the stranger, that join themselves to the Lord, to serve him, and to love the name of the Lord, to be his servants, every one that keepeth the sabbath from polluting it, and taketh hold of my covenant; Even them will I bring to my holy mountain, and make them joyful in my house of prayer: their burnt offerings and their sacrifices shall be accepted upon mine altar; for mine house shall be called an house of prayer for all people" (Isaiah 56:1-7).

Here in the book of Isaiah we read that God calls His house *"a house of prayer."* The Lord Jesus also taught the people of His day that the house of God was to be a house of prayer (Matthew 21:13; Mark 11:17; Luke 19:46). We must be praying in our churches to call them houses of prayer. Prayer should be the priority over everything else in the church, because it is only by prayer that our pastors are going to be men of God who will lead their congregations by the Holy Spirit of God. It is only by prayer that Sunday school teachers are going to teach effectively. It is only by prayer that converts are going to be added to the church and grow in grace and the knowledge of Jesus Christ. It is only by prayer that God's work is going to thrive effectively for His glory and reach our communities for Christ.

The definition of the word *Christian* means "to be like Christ," or "little Christ." Believers were first called Christians at Antioch because for the first time since the Savior's resurrection, there were some people who were closely mirroring the life of Christ. Do you act like Christ? The Lord Jesus Christ prayed. Let us follow the greatest example of prayer by following the life of the Lord Jesus Christ, studying His habits of prayer, then implementing those same habits into our own lives. A habit is something that is practiced so often it becomes usual behavior. The disciples knew that the Lord Jesus put a priority on prayer, so they said to Him, *"Lord, teach us to pray"* (Luke 11:1). If you follow the prayer life of our Lord Jesus and study it closely, you will find that anything He did was preceded by prayer. He prayed before He began His public ministry: *"Now when all the people were baptized, it came to pass, that Jesus also being baptized, and praying, the heaven was opened"* (Luke 3:21). Before He chose the twelve disciples whom he also called apostles, He prayed: *"He went out into a mountain to pray, and continued all night in prayer to God"* (Luke 6:12). We also find the Lord Jesus praying after He worked miracles: *"When he had sent the multitudes away, he went up into a mountain apart to pray: and when the evening was come, he was there alone"* (Matthew 14:23).

He did not forge ahead in the glory of the miracle, but rather sought His Father in prayer in order to be continually armed for the spiritual battle, and so that the devil would not be given any ground. Pride would be the natural recourse, and the Devil's delight, following such feats; however, that would rob God of His rightful glory. Praying before and after great acts of service renews the mind and spirit as well as strengthens the body and soul. The Lord Jesus was being refreshed and renewed by the Father in order to go and perform another miracle to the glory of God. (Read Matthew 14:22-31.)

As He had to be recharged and strengthened by the Father, so do we. Are you praying in this way? Most Christians are not, and it is evidenced in how little power there is in the church today. Many say, "He just got burned out," but actually what is happening is that men and women are continuing in their own strength instead of getting alone with God in prayer in order to be renewed and strengthened by the Holy Spirit to stay in the battle for Christ. In this day of cell phones, if we do not keep them charged they will run down and eventually stop working. As Christians we will run down and cease working for Christ if we are not continually being recharged through prayer. Daily prayer will give Christians daily strength, which will enable each one to continue laboring for Christ. If we would spend more time in prayer, just think of the power that God through His Holy Spirit could work through us!

HOW DO YOU LEARN TO PRAY?

You learn to pray by praying. If you are going to possess the power of God upon your Christian life and service you must learn to get alone with God and pray. *"But thou, when thou prayest, enter into thy closet, and when thou hast shut thy door, pray to thy Father which is in secret; and thy Father which seeth in secret shall reward thee openly"* (Matthew 6:6).

The Christian's vitality is found in prayer, alone with God, declaring complete dependency upon Him. *"He that dwelleth in the secret place of the most High shall abide under the shadow of the Almighty"* (Psalm 91:1).

The Lord Jesus continually humbled Himself before the Father even though He *"thought it not robbery to be equal with God"* (Philippians 2:6).

"And he went a little further, and fell on his face, and prayed, saying, O my Father, if it be possible, let this cup pass from me: nevertheless not as I will, but as thou wilt" (Matthew 26:39).

"And he was withdrawn from them about a stone's cast, and kneeled down, and prayed" (Luke 22:41).

Therefore, you are going to have to make humility your best friend if you will ever learn to pray.

"And the LORD appeared to Solomon by night, and said unto him, I have heard thy prayer, and have chosen this place to myself for

*an house of sacrifice. If I shut up heaven that there be no rain, or if I command the locusts to devour the land, or if I send pestilence among my people; If my people, which are called by my name, shall **humble themselves**, and pray, and seek my face, and turn from their wicked ways; then will I hear from heaven, and will forgive their sin, and will heal their land"* (II Chronicles 7:12-14).

Humble Yourself

God expects His people to humble themselves and pray: *"Humble yourselves in the sight of the Lord, and he shall lift you up"* (James 4:10).

Possessing the power in prayer that the Lord Jesus possessed means to clothe yourself in the garment of humility so that you may become humble in mind and heart. *"Likewise, ye younger, submit yourselves unto the elder. Yea, all of you be subject one to another, and be clothed with humility: for God resisteth the proud, and giveth grace to the humble"* (I Peter 5:5).

When you put on humility, then the body that is physically able will automatically follow, and you will show God the Father reverence by falling upon your knees, or laying prostrate upon your face, or at the very least, bowing your head in humble submission to Him.

God chose the weak to confound the mighty. God chose the foolish to confound the wise. If you look back on the history of the church, you will see that God saves the weak; God saves the foolish; God saves the wicked; God saves the harlot; and He confounds the mighty with it all. God specializes in taking the dull and making them sharp. Consider the great servants of God. God picked them up out of the alleys; He picked them up out of the beer gardens like he did with George Whitefield. God picked them up from an atheistic life like he did with R. A. Torrey. The world is fascinated by the way He changed them and made them new creatures in Christ.

"But God hath chosen the foolish things of the world to confound the wise; and God hath chosen the weak things of the world to confound the things which are mighty; and base things of the world, and things which are despised, hath God chosen, yea, and things which are not, to bring to nought things that are: that no flesh should glory in his presence" (I Corinthians 1:27-29).

It is in our weakness that we are made strong through the power of the Lord. We must remember from where we came. We were born in sin, and it was by the power of the blood of Jesus Christ that we were redeemed and given the ability to go to the Father. Therefore, when we pray, we must humble ourselves before Him.

PRAY ALWAYS

Daniel is an example of a man who prayed regardless of adverse circumstances.

"Then said these men, We shall not find any occasion against this Daniel, except we find it against him concerning the laws of his God. Then these presidents and princes assembled together to the king, and said thus unto him, King Darius, live for ever. All the presidents of the kingdom, the governors, and the princes, the counsellors, and the captains, have consulted together to establish a royal statute, and to make a firm decree, that whosoever shall ask a petition of any God or man for thirty days, save of thee, O king, he shall be cast into the den of lions. Now, O king, establish the decree, and sign the writing, that it be not changed, according to the law of the Medes and Persians, which altereth not.... Now when Daniel knew that the writing was signed, he went into his house; and his windows being open in his chamber toward Jerusalem, he kneeled upon his knees three

times a day, and prayed, and gave thanks before his God, as he did aforetime" (Daniel 6:5-10).

Daniel was not a panic-pray-er, he was a permanent pray-er. He prayed all the time. Daniel knew that the king had signed the decree; however, Daniel continued to pray as he had always done. He did not yield to fear of what man could do to him; rather, he continued obediently in prayer to God.

I was once asked, "If you had to give up your Bible or your prayer life, which would you give up?" I told them that I would give up my Bible. I can live for God without a Bible. That has been proven so often. The first time I went to Romania, they had not had a Bible in 50 years, and those people were living for God beyond what you and I can imagine living for God. You and I can live for God without a Bible, but I promise you, we could not live for Him if we could not talk to Him.

"Casting all your care upon him; for he careth for you" (1 Peter 5:7). We cast our burdens upon the Lord by prayer. I cannot emphasize enough that we will never know how to pray until we first get alone with God and begin to pray. If we pray, we won't give up. "And he spake a parable unto them to this end, that men ought always to pray, and not to faint" (Luke 18:1). Praying always means that we pray about everything, in all situations, every day and night.

MAKE SURE YOU'RE RIGHT WITH GOD

In order to pray for others, you must be sure your own heart is clean before God; therefore, when you begin to pray, allow God to search your heart. If He brings to your mind something that you need to confess and make right, do it; then you can pray, *"Search me, O God, and know my heart: try me, and know my thoughts: and see if there be any wicked way in me, and lead me in the way everlasting"* (Psalm 139:23-24).

If we know we have wronged someone and refuse to make it right, our fellowship with God will be hindered: "But your iniquities have separated between you and your God, and your sins have hid his face from you, that he will not hear" (Isaiah 59:2).

In order to effectively pray for others, we must be right before God in our own hearts and lives so that He will hear us.

LESSON TWO

THE PRIORITY OF PRAYER QUESTIONS

1. How many times is prayer mentioned in the Bible?

_____

_____

2. What does God call the house of prayer? Give a verse to back up your answer.

_____

_____

3. What is the definition of the word Christian?

_____

_____

4. What did Christ do before He did anything? Give two references to back up your answer.

_____

_____

5. Why is it important to pray before and after great acts of service?

_____

_____

6. Why is it that Christians so often get "burned out" in the Christian life?

_____

_____

7. How does a person learn to pray?

_____

_____

8. What is the best way to come before God? Give two references.

_____

_____

9. Give two examples of how we can show humility while praying.

_____

_____

10. What types of people does God often choose?

_____

_____

11. What was the key factor in Daniel's prayer life?

_____

_____

12. Can we serve God without having a Bible? Explain your answer.

_____

_____

13. What will keep us from fainting (giving up) in our Christian life?

_____

_____

14. If we are going to pray for others, what do we need to make sure of in our own lives?

_____

_____

THE WONDER OF PRAYER
(PART 1)

INTRODUCTION

Throughout the Bible, God talks about continual prayer. I want to call your attention to the wonder of prayer. You know, it is an absolute wonder that God would allow us to talk to Him. Why would He allow us to talk to Him? Why would He give us an audience with Him? Why would God make a way so that we could come to His throne of grace and find help in the time of need?

It is wonderful that it does not take God forever to answer prayer. He can answer immediately. He doesn't always, but the Bible says that He is a present help in the time of trouble. *"God is our refuge and strength, a very present help in trouble"* (Psalm 46:1). *"From the end of the earth will I cry unto thee, when my heart is overwhelmed: lead me to the rock that is higher than I"* (Psalm 61:2). *"And that Rock was Christ"* (I Corinthians 10:4c). It is through the Lord Jesus Christ that we are given access to God's throne of grace, and it is wonderful!

GOD ALLOWS US TO ASK FOR ANYTHING

It is wonderful to know that God's ability to care for you does not depend on your ability at all. You and I cannot ask anything so big that He cannot do it. He is in control of everything.

"And he said unto them, Which of you shall have a friend, and shall go unto him at midnight, and say unto him, Friend, lend me three loaves; for a friend of mine in his journey is come to me, and I have nothing to set before him? And he from within shall answer and say, Trouble me not: the door is now shut, and my children are with me in bed; I cannot rise and give thee. I say unto you, Though he will not rise and give him, because he is his friend, yet because of his importunity he will rise and give him as many as he needeth. And I say unto you, Ask, and it shall be given you; seek, and ye shall find; knock, and it shall be opened unto you. For every one that asketh receiveth; and he that seeketh findeth; and to him that knocketh it shall be opened. If a son shall ask bread of any of you that is a father, will he give him a stone? Or if he ask a fish, will he for a fish give him a serpent? Or if he shall ask an egg, will he offer him a scorpion? If ye then, being evil, know how to give good gifts unto your children: how much more shall your heavenly Father give the Holy Spirit to them that ask him?" (Luke 11:5-13)

It is possible that we might ask for something to satisfy our own selfish gain; therefore, though we ask, we can be sure that we will not receive. *"Ye ask, and receive not, because ye ask amiss, that ye may consume it upon your lusts"* (James 4:3).

But God does want you to ask. The word *ask* means "to continually ask."

"And he spake a parable unto them to this end, that men ought always to pray, and not to faint; saying, There was in a city a judge, which feared not God, neither regarded man: and there was a widow in that city; and she came unto him, saying, Avenge me of mine adversary. And he would not for a while: but after-

ward he said within himself, Though I fear not God, nor regard man; yet because this widow troubleth me, I will avenge her, lest by her continual coming she weary me. And the Lord said, Hear what the unjust judge saith. And shall not God avenge his own elect, which cry day and night unto him, though he bear long with them?" (Luke 18:1-7)

God is able, and He desires to answer your prayers. We must, like Abraham and others that we read about in the Bible, be willing to continue asking until He answers.

GOD IS ALWAYS THERE

Regardless of the time of day or night, God is always ready to hear our prayers. You may go to Him and pray at midnight or 3 o'clock in the morning; He is there. You will never have to wait on Him to meet with you; He is always waiting for you to come to Him. The wonder of prayer is that God committed Himself to always be available for you and me. He desires for us to come to Him and pray. The Psalmist David said, *"I cried unto the LORD with my voice, and he heard me out of his holy hill. Selah"* (Psalm 3:4).

"Praise waiteth for thee, O God, in Sion: and unto thee shall the vow be performed. O thou that hearest prayer, unto thee shall all flesh come" (Psalm 65:1-2).

GOD LISTENS TO CHILDREN

Another wonder of prayer is that God listens to children.

"Jesus called them unto him, and said, Suffer little children to come unto me, and forbid them not: for of such is the kingdom of God. Verily I say unto you, Whosoever shall not receive the kingdom of God as a little child shall in no wise enter therein" (Luke 18:16-17).

Little children keep asking for something again and again until they receive what they desire. God wants us to be like that and continue asking until we receive what we desire.

> *"And God heard the voice of the lad; and the angel of God called to Hagar out of heaven, and said unto her, What aileth thee, Hagar? fear not; for God hath heard the voice of the lad where he is. Arise, lift up the lad, and hold him in thine hand; for I will make him a great nation. And God opened her eyes, and she saw a well of water; and she went, and filled the bottle with water, and gave the lad drink. And God was with the lad; and he grew, and dwelt in the wilderness, and became an archer. And he dwelt in the wilderness of Paran: and his mother took him a wife out of the land of Egypt"* (Genesis 21:17-21).

CHILDREN ARE SPECIAL IN THE SIGHT OF GOD
The Gospels of Mark and Luke record that Jesus welcomed children to come to Him (Mark 10:14; Luke 18:16).

> *"At the same time came the disciples unto Jesus, saying, Who is the greatest in the kingdom of heaven? And Jesus called a little child unto him, and set him in the midst of them, and said, Verily I say unto you, Except ye be converted, and become as little children, ye shall not enter into the kingdom of heaven. Whosoever therefore shall humble himself as this little child, the same is greatest in the kingdom of heaven. And whoso shall receive one such little child in my name receiveth me. But whoso shall offend one of these little ones which believe in me, it were better for him that a millstone were hanged about his neck, and that he were drowned in the depth of the sea. Woe unto the world because of offences! for it must needs be that offences come; but woe to that man by whom*

the offence cometh! Wherefore if thy hand or thy foot offend thee, cut them off, and cast them from thee: it is better for thee to enter into life halt or maimed, rather than having two hands or two feet to be cast into everlasting fire. And if thine eye offend thee, pluck it out, and cast it from thee: it is better for thee to enter into life with one eye, rather than having two eyes to be cast into hell fire. Take heed that ye despise not one of these little ones; for I say unto you, That in heaven their angels do always behold the face of my Father which is in heaven" (Matthew 18:1-10).

How wonderful to know that God is listening to the prayers of children! We remember that God's ear is open to children; therefore, we must be careful not to minimize the importance of their prayers. When we go to the Father in prayer, we need to go with the faith of a child.

"Jesus called them unto him, and said, Suffer little children to come unto me, and forbid them not: for of such is the kingdom of God. Verily I say unto you, Whosoever shall not receive the kingdom of God as a little child shall in no wise enter therein" (Luke 18:16-17).

Pray for a City

Another thing you can pray for is a city. Jesus wept over a city. He said:

"O Jerusalem, Jerusalem, thou that killest the prophets, and stonest them which are sent unto thee, how often would I have gathered thy children together, even as a hen gathereth her chickens under her wings, and ye would not!" (Matthew 23:37)

Oh, He wanted to wrap them in His arms. He wanted to love them to Himself. He wanted to bring them to where the blessings were, to where they would be cared for in His covering. The Lord Jesus wept over that city. Have you ever wept over a city? Our cities today are in need of our prayers!

PRAY FOR A COUNTRY

Have you ever wept over a country? Daniel cried out to God for a country, confessing his sins and theirs. He said:

"And I set my face unto the Lord God, to seek by prayer and supplications, with fasting, and sackcloth, and ashes: and I prayed unto the LORD my God, and made my confession, and said, O Lord, the great and dreadful God, keeping the covenant and mercy to them that love him, and to them that keep his commandments; we have sinned, and have committed iniquity, and have done wickedly, and have rebelled, even by departing from thy precepts and from thy judgments: neither have we hearkened unto thy servants the prophets, which spake in thy name to our kings, our princes, and our fathers, and to all the people of the land. O Lord, righteousness belongeth unto thee, but unto us confusion of faces, as at this day; to the men of Judah, and to the inhabitants of Jerusalem, and unto all Israel, that are near, and that are far off, through all the countries whither thou hast driven them, because of their trespass that they have trespassed against thee. O Lord, to us belongeth confusion of face, to our kings, to our princes, and to our fathers, because we have sinned against thee. To the Lord our God belong mercies and forgivenesses, though we have rebelled against him; neither have we obeyed the voice of the LORD our God, to walk in his laws, which he set before us by his servants the prophets. Yea, all Israel have transgressed thy law, even by departing, that they might not obey thy voice; therefore the curse is poured upon us, and the oath

that is written in the law of Moses the servant of God, because we have sinned against him. And he hath confirmed his words, which he spake against us, and against our judges that judged us, by bringing upon us a great evil: for under the whole heaven hath not been done as hath been done upon Jerusalem. As it is written in the law of Moses, all this evil is come upon us: yet made we not our prayer before the L<small>ORD</small> our God, that we might turn from our iniquities, and understand thy truth" (Daniel 9:3-13).

That is where America is today. We have not obeyed God as we should. We have not listened to His Word. We have not walked according to Scripture, because we have not wept for our nation. We have not fervently sought to bring others into the house of God through many tears and prayers.

"He that goeth forth and weepeth, bearing precious seed, shall doubtless come again with rejoicing, bringing his sheaves with him" (Psalm 126:6).

The leaders of the nation are not the problem. Our homes and our churches are the problem. As the home goes, so goes the church. As the church goes, so goes the nation. Most homes do not even have a family altar anymore where they read the Bible and pray together.

PRAY FOR THE WORLD

Do you pray for the world? The following is one of several sayings the Lord has graciously given me: By prayer I can penetrate the jungles, reach out to the islands, cross the oceans, visit the hospitals, comfort the widows and orphans, encourage the hurting, lift up the fallen, encompass the world and never leave my closet. The Lord Jesus told His disciples, *"Pray ye therefore the Lord of the harvest, that he will send forth labourers into his harvest"* (Matthew 9:38).

Pray for a city, pray for a state, pray for a nation, pray for a world that is lost and in need of God, and that needs to be redeemed through the blood of the Lord Jesus Christ.

LESSON THREE

THE WONDER OF PRAYER QUESTIONS
PART 1

1. How is it that we are able to come before God?

_____

_____

2. What does God allow us to ask in prayer?

_____

_____

3. What is one way that God will not answer our prayer?

_____

_____

4. How often does God want us to ask for something?

_____

_____

5. Give an example of someone in the Bible who continued to ask until God answered the prayer.

_____

_____

6.   Is there ever a time that you cannot go to God in prayer?

_____

_____

7.   God answers the prayers of children. Give an example from the Bible where God heard the voice of a child.

_____

_____

8.   What characteristic does a child have that we should have when bowing in prayer?

_____

_____

9.   Give an example of someone in the Bible who prayed for his city.

_____

_____

10.   State two things that Daniel did when praying for his nation.

_____

_____

11.   What is one thing that can move the heart of God when we earnestly pray?

_____

_____

THE WONDER OF PRAYER (PART 2)

PRAY FOR AN INDIVIDUAL

*"And I [Moses] fell down before the LORD, as at the first, forty days and forty nights: I did neither eat bread, nor drink water, because of all your sins which ye sinned, in doing wickedly in the sight of the LORD to provoke him to anger. For I was afraid of the anger and hot displeasure, wherewith the LORD was wroth against you to destroy you. But the LORD hearkened unto me at that time also. And the LORD was very angry with Aaron to have destroyed him: and **I prayed for Aaron also the same time**"* (Deuteronomy 9:18-20).

M oses prayed for all the people, but He also prayed for one specific individual—Aaron. The Bible says, *"For what is a man profited, if he shall gain the whole world, and lose his own soul? or what shall a man give in exchange for his soul?"* (Matthew 16:26). Read also Mark 8:36 and Luke 9:25. One soul to Almighty God is worth more than all the wealth of the world combined.

"How think ye? if a man have an hundred sheep, and one of them be gone astray, doth he not leave the ninety and nine, and goeth into the mountains, and seeketh that which is gone astray? And

if so be that he find it, verily I say unto you, he rejoiceth more of that sheep, than of the ninety and nine which went not astray" (Matthew 18:12-13).

The Lord Jesus Himself set the example for us to pray for an individual when He prayed for Simon Peter.

"And the Lord said, Simon, Simon, behold, Satan hath desired to have you, that he may sift you as wheat: But I have prayed for thee, that thy faith fail not: and when thou art converted, strengthen thy brethren" (Luke 22:31-32).

In your praying it is imperative that you do not forget the individual. George Mueller, the great man of faith, prayed 55 years for one specific man to be saved; however, that man did not get saved until two years after George Mueller's death. Even though the man did not get saved in George Mueller's lifetime, God heard George Mueller's prayers and wonderfully saved the man. **Do not forget to pray for the individual!**

When we pray for someone, we need to learn to love them for who they are, not for what we think they should be. When we begin to love them like Christ loved us, we will be better able to pray for them without judgment. If we ever hope to help someone turn from the bondage of sin, we cannot despise them for where they presently are in sin. We do not love their sin; we love them like Jesus loved us. "But God commendeth his love toward us, in that, while we were yet sinners, Christ died for us" (Romans 5:8). God and His Son, Jesus Christ, loved us unconditionally when we were still in sin.

GOD CAN DO ANYTHING

"Then spake Joshua to the LORD in the day when the LORD delivered up the Amorites before the children of Israel, and he said in the sight of Israel, Sun, stand thou still upon Gibeon; and thou,

Moon, in the valley of Ajalon. And the sun stood still, and the moon stayed, until the people had avenged themselves upon their enemies. Is not this written in the book of Jasher? So the sun stood still in the midst of heaven, and hasted not to go down about a whole day. And there was no day like that before it or after it, that the LORD hearkened unto the voice of a man: for the LORD fought for Israel" (Joshua 10:12-14).

We may not understand these wonders of prayer, but the more we think on what God has done in answer to prayer, the more we will pray.

EFFECTUAL FERVENT PRAYER

"Confess your faults one to another, and pray one for another, that ye may be healed. The effectual fervent prayer of a righteous man availeth much. Elias was a man subject to like passions as we are, and he prayed earnestly that it might not rain: and it rained not on the earth by the space of three years and six months" (James 5:16-17).

The word "fervent," in the Greek, literally means heat to the boiling point, which is where we get our English word "fever." It figuratively means to be zealous. Thus, it is important to pray with fervency—with a burning desire that stems from deep within the heart. In essence you are saying to God that what you are praying for is something extremely necessary in order to glorify Him, lift up His name, and exalt Jesus Christ. Elijah was made of sinful flesh just like you and me, but he earnestly prayed for God to demonstrate His glory in answer to prayer. When you pray, remember that it is the effectual fervent prayer of a righteous man that will avail much. Therefore, when you pray, believe that you **will** receive. Be willing to say as did the apostle Paul, *"I believe God"* (Acts 27:25).

Understand to whom you are praying. It's a shame that more times than not we go to God in prayer about something without the faith to believe He **will** do it. He has promised over and over again in His Word that He **will** do it! *"And all things, whatsoever ye shall ask in prayer, believing, ye shall receive"* (Matthew 21:22). *"And whatsoever ye shall ask in my name, that will I do, that the Father may be glorified in the Son"* (John 14:13).

KEEP PRAYING

"Peter therefore was kept in prison: but prayer was made without ceasing of the church unto God for him. And when Herod would have brought him forth, the same night Peter was sleeping between two soldiers, bound with two chains: and the keepers before the door kept the prison. And, behold, the angel of the Lord came upon him, and a light shined in the prison: and he smote Peter on the side, and raised him up, saying, Arise up quickly. And his chains fell off from his hands. And the angel said unto him, Gird thyself, and bind on thy sandals. And so he did. And he saith unto him, Cast thy garment about thee, and follow me. And he went out, and followed him; and wist not that it was true which was done by the angel; but thought he saw a vision. When they were past the first and the second ward, they came unto the iron gate that leadeth unto the city; which opened to them of his own accord: and they went out, and passed on through one street; and forthwith the angel departed from him. And when Peter was come to himself, he said, Now I know of a surety, that the Lord hath sent his angel, and hath delivered me out of the hand of Herod, and from all the expectation of the people of the Jews. And when he had considered the thing, he came to the house of Mary the mother of John, whose surname was Mark; where

many were gathered together praying. And as Peter knocked at the door of the gate, a damsel came to hearken, named Rhoda. And when she knew Peter's voice, she opened not the gate for gladness, but ran in, and told how Peter stood before the gate. And they said unto her, Thou art mad. But she constantly affirmed that it was even so. Then said they, It is his angel. But Peter continued knocking: and when they had opened the door, and saw him, they were astonished. But he, beckoning unto them with the hand to hold their peace, declared unto them how the Lord had brought him out of the prison. And he said, Go shew these things unto James, and to the brethren. And he departed, and went into another place (Acts 12:5-17).

We see that the church continued praying for Peter's deliverance from prison. When you begin to pray about something, then continue praying about it until you receive God's answer. We can compare it to the account of Elisha and to Joash, king of Israel:

"And he said, Take the arrows. And he took them. And he said unto the king of Israel, Smite upon the ground. And he smote thrice, and stayed. And the man of God was wroth with him, and said, Thou shouldest have smitten five or six times; then hadst thou smitten Syria till thou hadst consumed it: whereas now thou shalt smite Syria but thrice" (II Kings 13:18-19).

We must not stop praying! The miraculous answer from the Lord will come, but we will not behold it if we stop praying.

Daniel's prayer life is another example of the importance of continuing to pray.

"Then said he [the messenger that God sent] unto me, Fear not, Daniel: for from the first day that thou didst set thine heart to

understand, and to chasten thyself before thy God, thy words were heard, and I am come for thy words. But the prince of the kingdom of Persia withstood me one and twenty days: but, lo, Michael, one of the chief princes, came to help me; and I remained there with the kings of Persia. Now I am come to make thee understand what shall befall thy people in the latter days: for yet the vision is for many days" (Daniel 10:12-14).

The answer to Daniel's prayer was sent immediately, but the Devil fought hard against it. We must not quit praying!

For twelve long years I prayed and wept to God for my daddy's salvation. The long-awaited answer arrived one night when my daddy woke up my godly mother and asked her, "Do you believe what Tommy preaches is the truth?"

"You know it is; that's why you are awake," was her response.

It was then, at midnight, that my daddy rolled out of bed, kneeled down and asked Jesus Christ to save Him. He was 75 years old when he got saved, and he lived another 20 years, singing praises to Jesus, telling others about Jesus, and rejoicing in his salvation. He wrote a note before he died, asking that there be one minute spent talking about him, and 59 minutes spent talking about the greatness of His Saviour. God is able to save and make all who come to Him new creatures in Christ; therefore, we must not stop, but continue praying.

The prophet Samuel said, *"Moreover as for me, God forbid that I should sin against the LORD in ceasing to pray for you..."* (I Samuel 12:23).

It is sin to stop praying for an individual, for a city, for a state, for a nation, for the world, or for anything. It doesn't matter how impossible the situation may appear, we must not sin by ceasing to pray.

LESSON FOUR

THE WONDER OF PRAYER QUESTIONS
PART 2

    1.   Give an example of someone in the Bible who prayed for an individual.

_____

_____

    2.   How important is one soul? Back up your answer with a verse.

_____

_____

    3.   What must we do if we are going to pray for someone?

_____

_____

    4.   To what extent are we to love someone?

_____

_____

    5.   Give a verse that shows us God loves us just the way we are.

_____

_____

6. What will help us begin to pray more?

_____

_____

7. What is the most effective way to pray?

_____

_____

8. What does the word *"fervent"* mean?

_____

_____

9. How must we come to God in prayer in order to receive the promise of Him answering our prayer?

_____

_____

10. What does it show God when we continue to pray for something specifically?

_____

_____

11. Give a verse stating that it is a sin to stop praying for someone.

_____

_____

THE WORK OF PRAYER

INTRODUCTION

P RAYING THE BIBLE way is going to take some work. If you are going to pray like Elijah—effectually and fervently—then you are going to have to labor in prayer. Very few people, however, will come to
the point where they are willing to agonize in prayer. When you fervently pray, you will come out of your place of prayer with puffy eyes
from weeping over those for whom you have been praying. You may
come away with your clothes and body wet with sweat from agonizing
over the thing you are praying about. It was said that John Hyde had so
fervently prayed for others, especially the nation of India where he was
a missionary, that his heart was physically affected. He had so prayed
that his heart was stretched across to the right side of his body at the
time of his death.

The Lord Jesus Christ effectually and fervently prayed.

*"Then cometh Jesus with them unto a place called Gethsemane,
and saith unto the disciples, Sit ye here, while I go and pray yon-
der. And he took with him Peter and the two sons of Zebedee,
and began to be sorrowful and very heavy"* (Matthew 26:36-37).

*"And being in an agony he prayed more earnestly: and his sweat was
as it were great drops of blood falling down to the ground"* (Luke 22:44).

The Savior had so agonized in prayer that an angel from heaven had to come and strengthen Him so that He could finish the work the Father had sent Him to do, which was to die on Calvary's cross for the sins of the world.

> *"And he was withdrawn from them about a stone's cast, and kneeled down, and prayed, saying, Father, if thou be willing, remove this cup from me: nevertheless not my will, but thine, be done"* (Luke 22:41-42).

The Lord Jesus was crying out in His prayer regarding the Father's will. You can never go any deeper than just wanting God's will. Many Christians talk about having a deeper life. My friend, you cannot get any deeper than wanting the will of God in your life.

WEEPING AND FASTING

In the Old Testament, in the book of First Samuel, there is an account of a lady named Hannah who fasted and wept in prayer to the Lord year after year.

> *"Now there was a certain man of Ramathaim-zophim, of mount Ephraim, and his name was Elkanah, the son of Jeroham, the son of Elihu, the son of Tohu, the son of Zuph, an Ephrathite: And he had two wives; the name of the one was Hannah, and the name of the other Peninnah: and Peninnah had children, but Hannah had no children. And this man went up out of his city yearly to worship and to sacrifice unto the LORD of hosts in Shiloh. And the two sons of Eli, Hophni and Phinehas, the priests of the LORD, were there. And when the time was that Elkanah offered, he gave to Peninnah his wife, and to all her sons and her daughters, portions: But unto Hannah he gave a worthy portion; for he loved Hannah: but the LORD had shut up her*

*womb. And her adversary also provoked her sore, for to make her fret, because the LORD had shut up her womb. And as he did so year by year, when she went up to the house of the LORD, so she provoked her; therefore she wept, and did not eat. **Then said Elkanah her husband to her, Hannah, why weepest thou? and why eatest thou not? and why is thy heart grieved? am not I better to thee than ten sons?** So Hannah rose up after they had eaten in Shiloh, and after they had drunk. Now Eli the priest sat upon a seat by a post of the temple of the LORD. And she was in bitterness of soul, and prayed unto the LORD, and wept sore"* (I Samuel 1:1-10).

Notice in the hightlighted verse that she was weeping and fasting. She was grieving so severely over her barren womb that she was in *"bitterness of soul"* and *"wept sore"* as she went to the Lord in prayer. It was apparent that she longed for a baby by the way that she was weeping, fasting, and grieving.

Hannah's barren womb had brought her such sorrow that she became broken with an insatiable longing for a baby. She had wept; she had fasted; she had grieved; and now with a sorrowful heart she was pouring out her soul about it to the Lord. She was emptying herself before the Lord, and that kind of praying requires work.

CONTINUING IN PRAYER

*"And she vowed a vow, and said, O LORD of hosts, if thou wilt indeed look on the affliction of thine handmaid, and remember me, and not forget thine handmaid, but wilt give unto thine handmaid a man child, then I will give him unto the LORD all the days of his life, and there shall no razor come upon his head. And it came to pass, as she **continued** praying before the LORD, that Eli marked her mouth. Now Hannah, she spake in her heart;*

only her lips moved, but her voice was not heard: therefore Eli thought she had been drunken. And Eli said unto her, How long wilt thou be drunken? put away thy wine from thee. And Hannah answered and said, No, my lord, I am a woman of a sorrowful spirit: I have drunk neither wine nor strong drink, but have poured out my soul before the LORD. Count not thine handmaid for a daughter of Belial: for out of the abundance of my complaint and grief have I spoken hitherto" (I Samuel 1:11-16).

Notice the highlighted word *continued*—a word in the Bible that it is often associated with praying. *"Persevere,"* *"without ceasing,"* and *"pray always"* are synonymous with *"continued."* Read the following verses: Luke 6:12; Luke 18:1; Luke 21:36; Acts 1:14; Acts 2:42; Acts 12:5; Romans 1:9; I Thessalonians 5:17.

WRESTLING IN PRAYER

There may be times when you will wrestle with God in prayer, and you will find that it is difficult work, but the rewards will be many. Jacob wrestled with God in prayer.

"And Jacob was left alone; and there wrestled a man with him until the breaking of the day. And when he saw that he prevailed not against him, he touched the hollow of his thigh; and the hollow of Jacob's thigh was out of joint, as he wrestled with him. And he said, Let me go, for the day breaketh. And he said, I will not let thee go, except thou bless me. And he said unto him, What is thy name? And he said, Jacob. And he said, Thy name shall be called no more Jacob, but Israel: for as a prince hast thou power with God and with men, and hast prevailed" (Genesis 32:24-28).

Wrestling in prayer means "getting alone with God" (*"And Jacob was left alone."*) —striving to get a hold of God and being determined to gain His favor and attention concerning a matter: *"And he said, I will not let thee go, except thou bless me."* We notice that *"Jacob's thigh was out of joint as he wrestled with him."* It is costly and painful to wrestle with God, but the dividends that we receive are worth it all. Jacob received a new walk. With his thigh being out of joint, he *"halted upon his thigh"* (Genesis 32:31b). He received a new name: *"And he said, Thy name shall be called no more Jacob, but Israel: for as a prince hast thou power with God and with men, and hast prevailed."* He also began writing a new history, for he no longer was living in the pride of his own heart, but in obedience to the will of God. When we wrestle with God in prayer, determined not to let go until we receive an answer from Him, then we can experience the reality of just how much we are dependent upon Him for everything.

The Work of Prayer in Soul-winning

Prayer is essential for every aspect of our life, which also includes winning souls to Christ.

> *"And he must needs go through Samaria. Then cometh he to a city of Samaria, which is called Sychar, near to the parcel of ground that Jacob gave to his son Joseph. Now Jacob's well was there. Jesus therefore, being wearied with his journey, sat thus on the well: and it was about the sixth hour.*
>
> *There cometh a woman of Samaria to draw water: Jesus saith unto her, Give me to drink. (For his disciples were gone away unto the city to buy meat.) Then saith the woman of Samaria unto him, How is it that thou, being a Jew, askest drink of me, which am a woman of Samaria? for the Jews have no dealings with the Samaritans.*

Jesus answered and said unto her, If thou knewest the gift of God, and who it is that saith to thee, Give me to drink; thou wouldest have asked of him, and he would have given thee living water.

The woman saith unto him, Sir, thou hast nothing to draw with, and the well is deep: from whence then hast thou that living water? Art thou greater than our father Jacob, which gave us the well, and drank thereof himself, and his children, and his cattle?

Jesus answered and said unto her, Whosoever drinketh of this water shall thirst again: But whosoever drinketh of the water that I shall give him shall never thirst; but the water that I shall give him shall be in him a well of water springing up into everlasting life.

The woman saith unto him, Sir, give me this water, that I thirst not, neither come hither to draw. Jesus saith unto her, Go, call thy husband, and come hither. The woman answered and said, I have no husband.

Jesus said unto her, Thou hast well said, I have no husband: For thou hast had five husbands; and he whom thou now hast is not thy husband: in that saidst thou truly.

The woman saith unto him, Sir, I perceive that thou art a prophet. Our fathers worshipped in this mountain; and ye say, that in Jerusalem is the place where men ought to worship.

Jesus saith unto her, Woman, believe me, the hour cometh, when ye shall neither in this mountain, nor yet at Jerusalem, worship the Father. Ye worship ye know not what: we know what we worship: for salvation is of the Jews. But the hour cometh, and now is, when the true worshippers shall worship the Father in spirit and in truth: for the Father seeketh such to worship him. God is a Spirit: and they that worship him must worship him in spirit and in truth.

The woman saith unto him, I know that Messias cometh, which is called Christ: when he is come, he will tell us all things.

Jesus saith unto her, I that speak unto thee am he. And upon this came his disciples, and marvelled that he talked with the woman: yet no man said, What seekest thou? or, Why talkest thou with her? The woman then left her waterpot, and went her way into the city, and saith to the men, Come, see a man, which told me all things that ever I did: is not this the Christ?" (John 4:4-29)

The Lord Jesus knew that woman would be at that particular well, which was why He needed to go through Samaria, because this woman needed to be saved. The Lord knows where to send you and who will be ready to hear the Gospel message.

"Who then is Paul, and who is Apollos, but ministers by whom ye believed, even as the Lord gave to every man? I have planted, Apollos watered; but God gave the increase" (I Corinthians 3:5-6).

He knows the hearts of people, and He is able to direct you by His Holy Spirit; therefore, before you go soul-winning—pray! While you are out soul-winning—pray! Allow the Lord to lead you through the Bible as you witness to people for Christ. Do not be dependent on any one set plan such as the Roman's Road, "Five Steps to Heaven," or any others; be dependent upon God by prayer. Believe that He will give you the Scripture verses to use, and that He will give you the words to say. If you will take time and study the life of the Lord Jesus Christ, you will find that when He spoke to individuals about salvation He did not tell any two the same thing. He told Nicodemus that he had to be born again: *"Jesus answered and said unto him, Verily, verily, I say unto thee, Except a man be born again, he cannot see the kingdom of God"* (John 3:3).

When the Lord Jesus spoke to Zacchaeus He never mentioned that he had to born again. *"And Jesus said unto him, This day is salvation come to this house, forsomuch as he also is a son of Abraham. For the Son of man is come to seek and to save that which was lost"* (Luke 19:9-10).

Ask God to fill your mouth with what the person needs to hear because what may affect one person may not affect another. In the matter of soul-winning, work at it—first with much prayer, then with tears, pleading from the heart. Ask God for souls, and then expect Him to answer and to give the increase in His time. *"He that goeth forth and weepeth, bearing precious seed, shall doubtless come again with rejoicing, bringing his sheaves with him"* (Psalm 126:6).

LESSON FIVE

THE WORK OF PRAYER QUESTIONS

1. What does it mean to agonize in prayer?

_____

_____

2. How does the Bible describe the fervency and agony of our Savior's prayers in the Garden of Gethsemane?

_____

_____

3. What is the deepest thing you can want for your life?

_____

_____

4. What did Hannah do to show how serious she was about her request?

_____

_____

5. How often did Hannah pray for a child?

_____

_____

6. Who wrestled in prayer?

_____

_____

7. What does it mean to wrestle in prayer?

_____

_____

8. Why is it important to be in prayer while soul-winning?

_____

_____

9. Give two examples from the Bible of someone getting saved.

_____

_____

10. Does everyone get saved the same way? Explain your answer.

_____

_____

11. Give the 5 steps you should take before you go out soul-winning.

_____

_____

THE HUMILITY OF PRAYER

INTRODUCTION

Humility is vastly important in the Christian's life. The Bible is very clear that as Christians, we need to humble ourselves: *"Humble yourselves in the sight of the Lord, and he shall lift you up"* (James 4:10).

> *"Likewise, ye younger, submit yourselves unto the elder. Yea, all of you be subject one to another, and be clothed with humility: for God resisteth the proud, and giveth grace to the humble. Humble yourselves therefore under the mighty hand of God, that he may exalt you in due time"* (I Peter 5:5-6).

> *"If my people, which are called by my name, shall humble themselves, and pray, and seek my face, and turn from their wicked ways; then will I hear from heaven, and will forgive their sin, and will heal their land"* (II Chronicles 7:14).

The humbler we become, the more we will go to the Lord in prayer, because humility heightens our awareness of God's great ability and our inability to do anything apart from Him.

CHRIST'S HUMILITY IN HIS VISAGE

The Lord Jesus Christ was not extraordinarily handsome; rather, He was common and ordinary-looking. His looks were so common that Judas had to kiss His cheek in order for the soldiers to be able to identify Him as Jesus Christ. *"But Jesus said unto him, Judas, betrayest thou the Son of man with a kiss?"* (Luke 22:48).

The Old Testament describes His appearance: *"For he shall grow up before him as a tender plant, and as a root out of a dry ground: he hath no form nor comeliness; and when we shall see him, there is no beauty that we should desire him"* (Isaiah 53:2).

The apostle John's description of how Jesus appeared in Heaven was as *"a Lamb as it had been slain"* (Revelation 5:6b).

It was not His physical appearance that attracted so many to Him; rather, it was His spirit of humility that drew people unto Him.

Christ's Humility in Reputation

"He is despised and rejected of men; a man of sorrows, and acquainted with grief: and we hid as it were our faces from him; he was despised, and we esteemed him not" (Isaiah 53:3). Jesus was despised and rejected not only by men, but by His very own people, for the Hebrew nation rejected Him. His own family initially did not believe Him. *"He came unto his own, and his own received him not"* (John 1:11). The city of Nazareth, where He was raised, rejected Him.

> *"And he came to Nazareth, where he had been brought up: and, as his custom was, he went into the synagogue on the sabbath day, and stood up for to read....And all they in the synagogue, when they heard these things, were filled with wrath, and rose up, and thrust him out of the city, and led him unto the brow of the hill whereon their city was built, that they might cast him down headlong"* (Luke 4:16, 28-29).

Jesus did not have the reputation of being wealthy. He did not even have a house of His own, and His clothing was made of the cheapest material. *"And Jesus saith unto him, The foxes have holes, and the birds of the air have nests; but the Son of man hath not where to lay his head"* (Matthew 8:20).

> *"And when he was come into his own country, he taught them in their synagogue, insomuch that they were astonished, and said, Whence hath this man this wisdom, and these mighty works? Is not this the carpenter's son? is not his mother called Mary? and his brethren, James, and Joses, and Simon, and Judas? And his sisters, are they not all with us? Whence then hath this man all these things? And they were offended in him. But Jesus said unto them, A prophet is not without honour, save in his own country, and in his own house"* (Matthew 13:54-57).

Jesus is the second Person in the Godhead. He is the Creator of Heaven and earth. He is the Son of God. However, when He came to earth to die for the sins of the world, He made Himself of no reputation:

> *"Who, being in the form of God, thought it not robbery to be equal with God: but made himself of no reputation, and took upon him the form of a servant, and was made in the likeness of men: and being found in fashion as a man, he humbled himself, and became obedient unto death, even the death of the cross"* (Philippians 2:6-8).

Jesus Christ became obedient to the death of the cross, which was the lowest form of death at the time. *"Christ hath redeemed us from the curse of the law, being made a curse for us: for it is written, Cursed is every one that hangeth on a tree"* (Galatians 3:13).

BOWING IN HUMILITY

Abraham sent his servant into his home country of Mesopotamia to find a wife for his son, Isaac. While the servant was there in

Abraham's homeland, he prayed to God to show him the right wife for Isaac. When God answered his prayer, he **bowed** his head and worshipped the Lord.

> "And Abraham was old, and well stricken in age: and the LORD had blessed Abraham in all things. And Abraham said unto his eldest servant of his house, that ruled over all that he had, Put, I pray thee, thy hand under my thigh: and I will make thee swear by the LORD, the God of heaven, and the God of the earth, that thou shalt not take a wife unto my son of the daughters of the Canaanites, among whom I dwell: but thou shalt go unto my country, and to my kindred, and take a wife unto my son Isaac....
>
> And he made his camels to kneel down without [outside] the city by a well of water at the time of the evening, even the time that women go out to draw water. And he said, O LORD God of my master Abraham, I pray thee, send me good speed this day, and shew kindness unto my master Abraham. Behold, I stand here by the well of water; and the daughters of the men of the city come out to draw water: and let it come to pass, that the damsel to whom I shall say, Let down thy pitcher, I pray thee, that I may drink; and she shall say, Drink, and I will give thy camels drink also: let the same be she that thou hast appointed for thy servant Isaac; and thereby shall I know that thou hast shewed kindness unto my master.
>
> And it came to pass, before he had done speaking, that, behold, Rebekah came out, who was born to Bethuel, son of Milcah, the wife of Nahor, Abraham's brother, with her pitcher upon her shoulder. And the damsel was very fair to look upon, a virgin, neither had any man known her: and she went down to the well, and filled her pitcher, and came up. And the servant ran to meet

her, and said, Let me, I pray thee, drink a little water of thy pitcher. And she said, Drink, my lord: and she hasted, and let down her pitcher upon her hand, and gave him drink. And when she had done giving him drink, she said, I will draw water for thy camels also, until they have done drinking. And she hasted, and emptied her pitcher into the trough, and ran again unto the well to draw water, and drew for all his camels.

And the man wondering at her held his peace, to wit whether the Lord had made his journey prosperous or not. And it came to pass, as the camels had done drinking, that the man took a golden earring of half a shekel weight, and two bracelets for her hands of ten shekels weight of gold; and said, Whose daughter art thou? tell me, I pray thee: is there room in thy father's house for us to lodge in?

*And she said unto him, I am the daughter of Bethuel the son of Milcah, which she bare unto Nahor. She said moreover unto him, We have both straw and provender enough, and room to lodge in. And the man **bowed** down his head, and worshipped the Lord. And he said, Blessed be the Lord God of my master Abraham, who hath not left destitute my master of his mercy and his truth: I being in the way, the Lord led me to the house of my master's brethren"* (Genesis 24:1-4, 11-27).

The servant **bowed** his head in humble gratitude before the Lord for having answered his prayer. God hears and answers the prayer of the humble. *"Lord, thou hast heard the desire of the humble: thou wilt prepare their heart, thou wilt cause thine ear to hear"* (Psalm 10:17).

"Then Moses called for all the elders of Israel, and said unto them, Draw out and take you a lamb according to your families, and kill the passover. And ye shall take a bunch of hyssop, and

dip it in the blood that is in the bason, and strike the lintel and the two side posts with the blood that is in the bason; and none of you shall go out at the door of his house until the morning. For the Lord will pass through to smite the Egyptians; and when he seeth the blood upon the lintel, and on the two side posts, the Lord will pass over the door, and will not suffer the destroyer to come in unto your houses to smite you. And ye shall observe this thing for an ordinance to thee and to thy sons for ever. And it shall come to pass, when ye be come to the land which the Lord will give you, according as he hath promised, that ye shall keep this service. And it shall come to pass, when your children shall say unto you, What mean ye by this service? That ye shall say, It is the sacrifice of the Lord's passover, who passed over the houses of the children of Israel in Egypt, when he smote the Egyptians, and delivered our houses. And the people bowed the head and worshipped" (Exodus 12:21-27).

At the reminder of what God did for them when they were in the land of Egypt, they bowed their heads and worshipped the Lord.

"And the Lord descended in the cloud, and stood with him there, and proclaimed the name of the Lord. And the Lord passed by before him, and proclaimed, The Lord, The Lord God, merciful and gracious, longsuffering, and abundant in goodness and truth, keeping mercy for thousands, forgiving iniquity and transgression and sin, and that will by no means clear the guilty; visiting the iniquity of the fathers upon the children, and upon the children's children, unto the third and to the fourth generation. And Moses made haste, and **bowed** *his head toward the earth, and worshipped"* (Exodus 34:5-8).

At one time, Moses was the Prince of Egypt, raised in the palace of Pharaoh. He was the general of Pharaoh's army, and the only man ever successful in defeating the capital city of Ethiopia. This is the same Moses who bowed his head in humility before the Lord.

KNEELING IN HUMILITY

Solomon was the king of Israel, and the Bible says that he was wiser than all men—I Kings 4:31. However, as he prayed before the elders of Israel, all the heads of the tribes of Israel, and all the congregation of Israel, he kneeled in humility. (Read I Kings chapter 8.)

> *"And it was so, that when Solomon had made an end of praying all this prayer and supplication unto the LORD, he arose from before the altar of the LORD, from **kneeling** on his knees with his hands spread up to heaven"* (I Kings 8:54).

Three positions demonstrate humility in prayer:

1) Standing with the head bowed
2) Kneeling
3) Lying prostrate on one's face

In this portion of Scripture, King Solomon is demonstrating humility by kneeling before God in prayer.

The prophet Ezra humbled himself before God:

> *"And at the evening sacrifice I arose up from my heaviness; and having rent my garment and my mantle, **I fell upon my knees**, and spread out my hands unto the LORD my God, and said, O my God, I am ashamed and blush to lift up my face to thee, my God: for our iniquities are increased over our head, and our trespass is grown up unto the heavens"* (Ezra 9:5-6).

We need to understand that we are talking to Almighty God when we are praying. He is the Creator! *"In the beginning God created the heaven and the earth"* (Genesis 1:1).

> *"Thus saith God the LORD, he that created the heavens, and stretched them out; he that spread forth the earth, and that which cometh out of it; he that giveth breath unto the people upon it, and spirit to them that walk therein"* (Isaiah 42:5).

When we pray, we are talking to the One who wonderfully and effortlessly created heaven and earth:

> *"By the word of the LORD were the heavens made; and all the host of them by the breath of his mouth. He gathereth the waters of the sea together as an heap: he layeth up the depth in storehouses. Let all the earth fear the LORD: let all the inhabitants of the world stand in awe of him. For he spake, and it was done; he commanded, and it stood fast"* (Psalm 33:6-9).

*"I have sworn by myself, the word is gone out of my mouth in righteousness, and shall not return, That unto me **every knee shall bow**, every tongue shall swear*[allegiance]*"* (Isaiah 45:23). One day every knee is going to bow before Him, Christians and non-Christians. Therefore, we need to demonstrate our reverence of Him and humble ourselves before Him when we pray.

THE LORD JESUS KNEELED

"And he [Jesus] *was withdrawn from them about a stone's cast, and **kneeled down**, and prayed"* (Luke 22:41). The eternal Son of God kneeled when He prayed. This is the greatest example of humility we could ever follow.

STEPHEN KNEELED

*"And he **kneeled** down, and cried with a loud voice, Lord, lay not this sin to their charge. And when he had said this, he fell asleep [died]"* (Acts 7:60).

THE APOSTLE PETER KNEELED

*"But Peter put them all forth, and **kneeled** down, and prayed; and turning him to the body said, Tabitha, arise. And she opened her eyes: and when she saw Peter, she sat up"* (Acts 9:40).

THE APOSTLE PAUL KNEELED

*"And when he had thus spoken, he **kneeled** down, and prayed with them all"* (Acts 20:36). *"And when we had accomplished those days, we departed and went our way; and they all brought us on our way, with wives and children, till we were out of the city: and we **kneeled** down on the shore, and prayed"* (Acts 21:5).

MOSES AND AARON KNEELED

"And Moses and Aaron went from the presence of the assembly unto the door of the tabernacle of the congregation, and they fell upon their faces: and the glory of the LORD appeared unto them" (Numbers 20:6).

JOSHUA KNEELED

"And he said, Nay; but as captain of the host of the LORD am I now come. And Joshua fell on his face to the earth, and did worship, and said unto him, What saith my lord unto his servant?" (Joshua 5:14).

ELIJAH KNEELED

"So Ahab went up to eat and to drink. And Elijah went up to the top of Carmel; and he cast himself down upon the earth, and put his face between his knees" (I Kings 18:42).

God knows whether or not we are physically able to kneel, and He understands if we physically cannot; but we must always humble ourselves before Him in prayer—whether in private or in public praying—by at least bowing our heads.

Lesson Six

The Humility of Prayer Questions

1. Why is humility so important?

_____

_____

2. How does God respond to those that humble themselves?

_____

_____

3. What are four things that Christians can do that will result in God healing our land?

_____

_____

4. Who is the perfect example of humility?

_____

_____

5. How did Jesus' appearance portray humility?

_____

_____

6. How did Jesus' reputation portray humility?

_____

_____

7. Give two references that show Jesus being rejected by man.

_____

_____

8. What are two positions we can have to show humility when praying?

_____

_____

9. What three positions in prayer are found in the Bible?

_____

_____

10. Give three examples of people who kneeled while praying.

_____

_____

HINDRANCES TO PRAYER

INTRODUCTION

THERE ARE HINDRANCES to prayer, and unconfessed sin is one that will turn God's ear away from hearing us. When we go to prayer, we need to ask God to reveal to us any hindrances there may be between us and Him, and whether or not there is sin in our heart that needs to be confessed. *"The heart is deceitful above all things, and desperately wicked: who can know it?"* (Jeremiah 17:9).

Before you pray, take time to examine your heart as David did: *"Search me, O God, and know my heart: try me, and know my thoughts: and see if there be any wicked way in me, and lead me in the way everlasting"* (Psalm 139:23-24).

> *"Be not rash with thy mouth, and let not thine heart be hasty to utter any thing before God: for God is in heaven, and thou upon earth: therefore let thy words be few"* (Ecclesiastes 5:2).

RELATIONAL HINDRANCES

If family relationships between one another are not right, then your prayer life will be hindered.

> *"Likewise, ye wives, be in subjection to your own husbands; that, if any obey not the word, they also may without the word be won by the conversation of the wives; while they behold your chaste*

conversation coupled with fear. Whose adorning let it not be that outward adorning of plaiting the hair, and of wearing of gold, or of putting on of apparel; but let it be the hidden man of the heart, in that which is not corruptible, even the ornament of a meek and quiet spirit, which is in the sight of God of great price. For after this manner in the old time the holy women also, who trusted in God, adorned themselves, being in subjection unto their own husbands: even as Sara obeyed Abraham, calling him lord: whose daughters ye are, as long as ye do well, and are not afraid with any amazement. Likewise, ye husbands, dwell with them according to knowledge, giving honour unto the wife, as unto the weaker vessel, and as being heirs together of the grace of life; that your prayers be not hindered" (I Peter 3:1-7).

Read Ephesians 5:21-33 and Ephesians 6:1-4. These portions of Scripture describe God's plan for unity in the home.

God has clearly told us from His Word how families are to live together. He has set forth a wonderful plan that if we will follow it, our prayers will not be hindered. When a wife takes the leadership role from her husband and does not respect him, her prayers will be hindered because she is not following the plan God designed. When husbands do not love their wives (meaning, they are not patient, kind, unselfish, humble and courteous to their wives), their prayers will be hindered. (Read I Corinthians 13:4-8.) When children are disobedient and disrespectful to their parents, then their prayers will be hindered. When fathers incite their children to undue anger in the way they treat them, then their prayers will be hindered. God is specific about the family unit and the way it is supposed to function; therefore, if we want to have an effective prayer life that is not hindered, we need to live with our families the way God planned.

INIQUITY HINDERS PRAYER

"If I regard iniquity in my heart, the Lord will not hear me" (Psalm 66:18). *Iniquity* is "unrighteousness, sin, transgression, committing wrong against God." The Bible says that sin starts in the heart, which is why we need to daily ask the Lord to search our hearts so that we may confess any sin and keep our hearts clean before Him. *"For out of the heart proceed evil thoughts, murders, adulteries, fornications, thefts, false witness, blasphemies"* (Matthew 15:19). *"For from within, out of the heart of men, proceed evil thoughts, adulteries, fornications, murders"* (Mark 7:21). *"Keep thy heart with all diligence; for out of it are the issues of life"* (Proverbs 4:23). It is the heart that prompts our thinking and leads us to carry out action. *"For as he thinketh in his heart, so is he: Eat and drink, saith he to thee; but his heart is not with thee"* (Proverbs 23:7).

Our thought processes, our actions, our fears, our anxieties, our responses all originate in our hearts; therefore, we need to keep a watch over our hearts so that they may remain clean and pure.

> *"But your iniquities have separated between you and your God, and your sins have hid his face from you, that he will not hear. For your hands are defiled with blood, and your fingers with iniquity; your lips have spoken lies, your tongue hath muttered perverseness"* (Isaiah 59:2-3).

We need to be careful what we do with our hands, and what we say with our tongues. Read the entire chapter of Isaiah 59.

"Then shall they cry unto the LORD, but he will not hear them: he will even hide his face from them at that time, as they have behaved themselves ill in their doings" (Micah 3:4). We need to be careful in our interactions with others so that we do not cheat anyone or enter into any crooked dealings if we do not want our prayers to be hindered.

"These six things doth the LORD hate: yea, seven are an abomination unto him: A proud look, a lying tongue, and hands that shed innocent blood, an heart that deviseth wicked imaginations, feet that be swift in running to mischief, a false witness that speaketh lies, and he that soweth discord among brethren" (Proverbs 6:16-19).

A COLD AND INDIFFERENT HEART HINDERS PRAYER

"Because I have called, and ye refused; I have stretched out my hand, and no man regarded; But ye have set at nought all my counsel, and would none of my reproof: I also will laugh at your calamity; I will mock when your fear cometh; when your fear cometh as desolation, and your destruction cometh as a whirlwind; when distress and anguish cometh upon you. Then shall they call upon me, but I will not answer; they shall seek me early, but they shall not find me: for that they hated knowledge, and did not choose the fear of the LORD: they would none of my counsel: they despised all my reproof. Therefore shall they eat of the fruit of their own way, and be filled with their own devices. For the turning away of the simple shall slay them, and the prosperity of fools shall destroy them. But whoso hearkeneth unto me shall dwell safely, and shall be quiet from fear of evil" (Proverbs 1:24-33).

In essence, God is telling them that because they wouldn't listen to Him, He wouldn't hear their prayers. God tried to correct them, but they chose their way. They behaved as though He was nowhere nearby. When they faced trials, they wanted Him to help them. Like the Israelites, when we harden our hearts and do not heed God when He speaks to us, we are expressing coldness toward God. He said that when this occurs, **"Then shall they call upon me, but I will not answer; they shall seek me early, but they shall not find me."**

"Wherefore (as the Holy Ghost saith, To day if ye will hear his voice, harden not your hearts, as in the provocation, in the day of temptation in the wilderness:...Take heed, brethren, lest there be in any of you an evil heart of unbelief, in departing from the living God. But exhort one another daily, while it is called To day; lest any of you be hardened through the deceitfulness of sin. For we are made partakers of Christ, if we hold the beginning of our confidence stedfast unto the end; while it is said, To day if ye will hear his voice, harden not your hearts, as in the provocation" (Hebrews 3:7-8, 12-15).*

It is the deceitfulness of sin that hardens the heart and makes our hearts cold toward God; therefore, beware of sin. Allowing one sin opens the way for another; and continued sinful acts can result in habits that turn our hearts away from the Lord. In order to keep from having a cold and indifferent heart it is imperative that we daily draw near to God. As we draw near to Him, He will draw near to us. Our hearts will remain yielded and tender to His will and way, and our prayers will not be hindered.

"Let us draw near with a true heart in full assurance of faith, having our hearts sprinkled from an evil conscience, and our bodies washed with pure water. Let us hold fast the profession of our faith without wavering; (for he is faithful that promised;) and let us consider one another to provoke unto love and to good works: Not forsaking the assembling of ourselves together, as the manner of some is; but exhorting one another: and so much the more, as ye see the day approaching" (Hebrews 10:22-25).

Young people and older people can yield to the Lord.

"Therefore Eli said unto Samuel, Go, lie down: and it shall be, if he call thee, that thou shalt say, Speak, LORD; for thy servant

heareth. So Samuel went and lay down in his place. And the LORD *came, and stood, and called as at other times, Samuel, Samuel. Then Samuel answered, Speak; for thy servant heareth"* (I Samuel 3:9-10).

"Also I heard the voice of the Lord, saying, Whom shall I send, and who will go for us? Then said I, Here am I; send me" (Isaiah 6:8).

If we will say with Samuel, **"Speak,** LORD**; for thy servant heareth,"** and say with Isaiah, **"Here am I,"** then our hearts will not become cold toward God, and our prayers will not be hindered.

DO NOT BECOME COLD AND INDIFFERENT TO THE CRY OF THE POOR

Do not let your heart become hardened to the needs of the homeless or to anyone less fortunate than you. If they call on you for help, then help them. Ask God to give you the compassion that the Lord Jesus Christ had for the poor. When we turn away from hearing the cry of the poor, then the Bible says our prayers will be hindered. *"Whoso stoppeth his ears at the cry of the poor, he also shall cry himself, but shall not be heard"* (Proverbs 21:13).

DO NOT BE COLD AND INDIFFERENT TO GOD'S COMMANDS.

"He that turneth away his ear from hearing the law, even his prayer shall be abomination" (Proverbs 28:9). The prayer of one who stubbornly disobeys God's commands will be an abomination to God. Therefore, we need to be careful to obey God's commands, to be teachable, to be a student of God's Word, and to study it faithfully so that we will not turn our ear away from hearing the law of God and thus hinder our praying. *"If ye abide in me, and my words abide in you, ye shall ask what ye will, and it shall be done unto you"* (John 15:7). If we would *"abide"*—be continually—in the Word of God and make application of

it in our lives, then we will be less likely to disobey God's commands, and our prayers will not be hindered.

Unteachable

Basically, God is saying, "If you won't listen to Me, I won't listen to you. If you are not interested in what I am trying to teach you, then I won't listen to you when you ask for something." That's what Abraham told the rich man in Hell. He said that if his brothers would not hear Moses and the prophets, neither would they believe someone who rose from the dead. It wouldn't make any difference. Read Luke 16:19-31. People ask why don't they bring the Ark off of Mt. Ararat and set it in New York at Times Square; think of all the people that would get saved. No, they wouldn't. People don't get saved by sight; they get saved by faith. They'd just make fun of it. When people become unteachable, they don't want to listen; therefore, God tells us to keep our heart and our mind open to Him. We are to love God with our mind, with our heart, and with our soul.

We can become hardened toward each other if we aren't careful. When that happens, husbands don't want to listen to their wives and wives don't want to listen to their husbands. Parents don't take time to listen to their children and children don't listen to their parents.

My mother had 14 children, but when I came home from school in the afternoon, she would sit down and set me on her lap and say, "Tommy, turn over to your work today." I'd turn to it in my writing tablet and she would look at it and read a little bit of it and say, "Oh my. You must be the smartest boy in the whole world." She took time with me and each of my siblings, letting us know how much she loved us. That's the way we need to be toward people. We need to have a kind heart. We need to be that way toward the Word of God. Every time somebody is preaching, open your Bible. Take notes every time.

Only 20 percent of what you learn comes from hearing. 80% of what you learn comes from seeing. That's why the television and computer are so influential. We need to take time for God to speak to us from His written Word as we study His Word, search His Word, and read His Word. *"Out of the abundance of the heart, the mouth speaketh"* (Matthew 12:34b). Whatever your heart is full of, your mouth will talk about. We need to understand that, and we need to get in the Bible and get the Bible in us. D. L. Moody said, "This Book will keep you from sin or sin will keep you from this Book." That's exactly right. The Lord Jesus said, *"If ye abide in me, and my words abide in you, ye shall ask what ye will, and it shall be done unto you"* (John 15:7).

We need to load ourselves with the Word of God. We need to be completely occupied with Christ. If we abide in Christ and His Word lives in us, then we will receive what we are asking for and our prayers will not be hindered.

NOT TELLING OTHERS

"When I say unto the wicked, Thou shalt surely die; and thou givest him not warning, nor speakest to warn the wicked from his wicked way, to save his life; the same wicked man shall die in his iniquity; but his blood will I require at thine hand" (Ezekiel 3:18).

"When I say unto the wicked, O wicked man, thou shalt surely die; if thou dost not speak to warn the wicked from his way, that wicked man shall die in his iniquity; but his blood will I require at thine hand" (Ezekiel 33:8).

When we do not warn others of eternal hell and tell them of God's saving grace through the blood of His Son, Jesus Christ, then our prayers can be hindered. If the Holy Spirit has impressed on you to witness to someone about the saving knowledge of Jesus Christ and you do not, then your prayers will be hindered.

"Wherefore I take you to record this day, that I am pure from the blood of all men. For I have not shunned to declare unto you all the counsel of God" (Acts 20:26-27). We need to be diligent to warn others of hell and tell them of salvation in Jesus Christ so that we do not hinder our prayers.

"Therefore it is come to pass, that as he cried, and they would not hear; so they cried, and I would not hear, saith the LORD of hosts" (Zechariah 7:13).

When the Spirit of God speaks to your heart to tell someone about Jesus Christ, you need to obey so that God will not turn away His ear from hearing your prayers.

UNBELIEF HINDERS PRAYER

When we pray we must believe the promises of God. We must believe we are talking to the One who alone can help and supply the need. We must believe God will do it! If we do not believe, then our prayers will be hindered. We do not have to have great faith, just faith in a great God. *"Jesus said unto him, If thou canst believe, all things are possible to him that believeth"* (Mark 9:23).

> *"But let him ask in faith, nothing wavering. For he that wavereth is like a wave of the sea driven with the wind and tossed. For let not that man think that he shall receive any thing of the Lord. A double minded man is unstable in all his ways"* (James 1:6-8).

UNFORGIVENESS HINDERS PRAYER

Be quick to forgive. Having a forgiving spirit will keep the prayer line open with God. *"For if ye forgive men their trespasses, your heavenly Father will also forgive you: but if ye forgive not men their trespass-*

es, neither will your Father forgive your trespasses" (Matthew 6:14-15). "And be ye kind one to another, tenderhearted, forgiving one another, even as God for Christ's sake hath forgiven you" (Ephesians 4:32).

"Then came Peter to him, and said, Lord, how oft shall my brother sin against me, and I forgive him? till seven times? Jesus saith unto him, I say not unto thee, Until seven times: but, Until seventy times seven" (Matthew 18:21-22).

LESSON SEVEN

HINDRANCES TO PRAYER QUESTIONS

1. Is there ever a time God does not hear your prayers? Explain your answer.

_____

_____

2. What should you do before you begin to pray?

_____

_____

3. Give a verse showing how family relationships can affect prayers.

_____

_____

4. What does a wife need to do in her role in the family?

_____

_____

5. What does a husband need to do in his role in the family?

_____

_____

6.   What is one thing a father might do toward his children that can hinder his prayers?

_____

_____

7.   What is iniquity?

_____

_____

8.   Where does sin start?

_____

_____

9.   How does a person become hardened toward God?

_____

_____

10.   What happens when a person becomes hardened toward God?

_____

_____

11.   Give a verse stating if we become cold toward the poor, God will not hear our prayers.

_____

_____

12. How can we avoid becoming disobedient to God's commands?

_____

_____

13. How does a person remain teachable?

_____

_____

14. What happens if we do not tell others about their sin?

_____

_____

15. Give a verse showing that unbelief hinders prayers.

_____

_____

16. How many times should you forgive someone?

_____

_____

The Holiness of Prayer (Part 1)

God Is Holy

"I will also praise thee with the psaltery, even thy truth, O my God: unto thee will I sing with the harp, O thou Holy One of Israel" (Psalm 71:22). The "O" in this verse is recognizing the Holiness of God.

> *"For I am the LORD your God: ye shall therefore sanctify yourselves, and ye shall be holy; for I am holy: neither shall ye defile yourselves with any manner of creeping thing that creepeth upon the earth. For I am the LORD that bringeth you up out of the land of Egypt, to be your God: ye shall therefore be holy, for I am holy"* (Leviticus 11:44-45).

> *"But as he which hath called you is holy, so be ye holy in all manner of conversation; because it is written, Be ye holy; for I am holy"* (I Peter 1:15-16).

GOD IS HOLY, and He requires His children to be holy. We can only be holy through His Holy Spirit who lives within us after we receive Jesus Christ as our Savior; therefore, we need to yield ourselves to the Holy Spirit and obey His leading so that we do not quench Him. We quench Him when we do not yield to and obey Him. The more we walk in the Spirit, which is saying "Yes" to Him, the more we will be controlled by the Spirit.

Read Psalm 99:9 and Exodus 15:11. God the Father is holy; His Son Jesus is holy; and His Spirit is holy. When the Lord Jesus resurrected and ascended up to Heaven, then the Father sent the Comforter, which is the Holy Spirit, and He dwells within every believer.

> *"And I will pray the Father, and he shall give you another Comforter, that he may abide with you for ever; even the Spirit of truth; whom the world cannot receive, because it seeth him not, neither knoweth him: but ye know him; for he dwelleth with you, and shall be in you…. But the Comforter, which is the Holy Ghost, whom the Father will send in my name, he shall teach you all things, and bring all things to your remembrance, whatsoever I have said unto you"* (John 14:16-17, 26).

If we are born-again believers in Jesus Christ, we are able to approach the Father in prayer because of the holiness of His Son and His Spirit. For through salvation in Jesus Christ we have been made one in Him so that the Father no longer sees our sinfulness, but the holy righteousness of His Son.

WHAT IS HOLINESS?

Holiness is "the absence of sin." *"That he might present it to himself a glorious church, not having spot, or wrinkle, or any such thing; but that it should be holy and without blemish"* (Ephesians 5:27).

> *"Forasmuch as ye know that ye were not redeemed with corruptible things, as silver and gold, from your vain conversation received by tradition from your fathers; but with the precious blood of Christ, as of a lamb without blemish and without spot"* (I Peter 1:18-19).

Not only does God not sin, but He does not have the possibility to sin, and that is holiness. *"For we have not an high priest which cannot be touched with the feeling of our infirmities; but was in all points tempted like as we are, yet without sin"* (Hebrews 4:15). *"There is none holy as the LORD: for there is none beside thee: neither is there any rock like our God"* (I Samuel 2:2).

"And he said, Draw not nigh hither: put off thy shoes from off thy feet, for the place whereon thou standest is holy ground" (Exodus 3:5). The ground on which Moses stood was holy because God was there. It was only holy ground because of God's presence. God is the source of all holiness, and without Him we cannot be holy in ourselves or in anything we do for Him.

HOLY REVERENCE TO GOD IN PRAYER

We need to be conscious of who we are addressing when we go to God in prayer. We are entering into the holy presence of Almighty God, our Heavenly Father—a privilege made possible through the holy righteousness of His Son, Jesus Christ, the second Person in the Godhead. His Holy Spirit then *"maketh intercession for us with groanings which cannot be uttered"* (Romans 8:26).

"And one cried unto another, and said, Holy, holy, holy, is the LORD of hosts: the whole earth is full of his glory" (Isaiah 6:3). The whole earth is filled with God's glory.

GOD WANTS US TO BE HOLY

"For I am the LORD your God: ye shall therefore sanctify yourselves, and ye shall be holy; for I am holy: neither shall ye defile yourselves with any manner of creeping thing that creepeth upon the earth. For I am the LORD that bringeth you up out of the land of Egypt, to be your God: ye shall therefore be holy, for I am holy" (Leviticus 11:44-45).

"But as he which hath called you is holy, so be ye holy in all manner of conversation" (I Peter 1:15).

We are not going to reach perfection in this life; however, we can *"press toward the mark"* by yielding to the will of the Father. (Read Philippians 3:9-14.) *"That he would grant unto us, that we being delivered out of the hand of our enemies might serve him without fear, in holiness and righteousness before him, all the days of our life"* (Luke 1:74-75).

God desires that we strive toward holiness so that our lives will be singularly lived for Him. Circumstances should not keep us from seeking to follow after God's holiness. We can look at examples of people in the Bible who did not let circumstances hinder them from following after God and holiness. The three Hebrew children and Daniel are some examples.

> *"Now if ye be ready that at what time ye hear the sound of the cornet, flute, harp, sackbut, psaltery, and dulcimer, and all kinds of musick, ye fall down and worship the image which I have made; well: but if ye worship not, ye shall be cast the same hour into the midst of a burning fiery furnace; and who is that God that shall deliver you out of my hands? Shadrach, Meshach, and Abednego, answered and said to the king, O Nebuchadnezzar, we are not careful to answer thee in this matter. If it be so, our God whom we serve is able to deliver us from the burning fiery furnace, and he will deliver us out of thine hand, O king. But if not, be it known unto thee, O king, that we will not serve thy gods, nor worship the golden image which thou hast set up"* (Daniel 3:15-18).

Mordecai refused to bow before Haman even though it was decreed that he do so. He could not serve both God and man, nor can we if we are seeking to live a holy life that is pleasing to Him.

"After these things did king Ahasuerus promote Haman the son of Hammedatha the Agagite, and advanced him, and set his seat above all the princes that were with him. And all the king's servants, that were in the king's gate, bowed, and reverenced Haman: for the king had so commanded concerning him. But Mordecai bowed not, nor did him reverence. Then the king's servants, which were in the king's gate, said unto Mordecai, Why transgressest thou the king's commandment? Now it came to pass, when they spake daily unto him, and he hearkened not unto them, that they told Haman, to see whether Mordecai's matters would stand: for he had told them that he was a Jew. And when Haman saw that Mordecai bowed not, nor did him reverence, then was Haman full of wrath. And he thought scorn to lay hands on Mordecai alone; for they had shewed him the people of Mordecai: wherefore Haman sought to destroy all the Jews that were throughout the whole kingdom of Ahasuerus, even the people of Mordecai" (Esther 3:1-6).

We need to understand that no matter what the circumstances, no matter what we are facing, no matter what trial is entering into our life, we should not stop striving after the holiness of God.

PERFECTING HOLINESS

"Having therefore these promises, dearly beloved, let us cleanse ourselves from all filthiness of the flesh and spirit, perfecting holiness in the fear of God" (II Corinthians 7:1). In the eyes of God, we become holy in Christ when we get saved because receiving Christ means we also receive His holiness. Therefore, in everything, may we yield to the Holy Spirit of Christ in us and not to the sinfulness of our flesh. *"Follow peace with all men, and holiness, without which no man shall see the Lord"* (Hebrews 12:14). People need to see God's peace and holiness

in our lives so that we may win them to Christ. *"Seeing then that all these things shall be dissolved, what manner of persons ought ye to be in all holy conversation and godliness"* (II Peter 3:11). God wants His children to walk holy, talk holy, live holy, and conduct ourselves with holiness in every area of our lives; and that can only be done through the power of the Holy Spirit of Christ.

LESSON EIGHT

THE HOLINESS OF PRAYER QUESTIONS
PART 1

1. By Whom can we become holy?

_____

_____

2. How do we become holy?

_____

_____

3. Why are we able to approach the Father in prayer?

_____

_____

4. What is holiness?

_____

_____

5. Is it possible for God to sin?

_____

_____

6.   What makes something holy?

_____

_____

7.   Give a Bible reference that shows us that God wants us to be holy.

_____

_____

8.   Give examples of people who did not let circumstances hinder them from following after God and holiness.

_____

_____

9.   How do we perfect holiness?

_____

_____

10.   Give a verse stating we can perfect holiness.

_____

_____

THE HOLINESS OF PRAYER (PART 2)

ABIDE IN HOLINESS

PSALM 15:1 SAYS, *"LORD, who shall abide in thy tabernacle? who shall dwell in thy holy hill?"* God is Almighty. He is the Lord of Hosts, Creator of the world and all that's in it. The word *abide* means "to live." David is saying, "Who is going to live in the tabernacle?"

I often think of Anna, the prophetess in the New Testament, who was a widow for 84 years. She had to be over 100 years old if she had been a widow for 84 years. She prayed day and night, which means that every day she went to the tabernacle and prayed and every night she went back to spend more time praying. (Read Luke 2:36-38.) In Psalm 15 David is asking God who will abide in His tabernacle. Who can live in His presence? Read the entire chapter of Psalm 15, and you will find the answers. God is a holy God, and nothing but holiness can abide (live) with Him.

GOD IS HOLY

The God of eternity is so holy that, in our human flesh, we cannot stand in His presence and live. It takes the holiness of His Son to clothe us in His righteousness and make it possible for us to go to God in prayer. When the apostle John was given the revelation of Jesus

Christ on the island of Patmos, he fell at the feet of Jesus as though he were dead. *"And when I saw him, I fell at his feet as dead. And he laid his right hand upon me, saying unto me, Fear not; I am the first and the last"* (Revelation 1:17).

Daniel couldn't stand before the holy presence of the Lord:

> *"And in the four and twentieth day of the first month, as I was by the side of the great river, which is Hiddekel; then I lifted up mine eyes, and looked, and behold a certain man clothed in linen, whose loins were girded with fine gold of Uphaz: His body also was like the beryl, and his face as the appearance of lightning, and his eyes as lamps of fire, and his arms and his feet like in colour to polished brass, and the voice of his words like the voice of a multitude. And I Daniel alone saw the vision: for the men that were with me saw not the vision; but a great quaking fell upon them, so that they fled to hide themselves. Therefore I was left alone, and saw this great vision, and there remained no strength in me: for my comeliness was turned in me into corruption, and I retained no strength"* (Daniel 10:4-8).

When the seraphims fly into God's presence they cover the only two naked places on their bodies—their faces and their feet. *"Above it stood the seraphims: each one had six wings; with twain he covered his face, and with twain he covered his feet, and with twain he did fly"* (Isaiah 6:2).

If we are going to draw closer to the Lord, we need to understand that He is a holy God, and the un-holiness of our flesh cannot stand before Him. However, the holiness of Jesus Christ in us allows us to enter the holy presence of God; therefore, we must strive to keep our hearts pure. *"Who shall ascend into the hill of the LORD? or who shall stand in his holy place? He that hath clean hands, and a pure heart; who hath not lifted up his soul unto vanity, nor sworn deceitfully"* (Psalm 24:3-4).

"Give unto the LORD the glory due unto his name: bring an offering, and come before him: worship the LORD in the beauty of holiness.... And say ye, Save us, O God of our salvation, and gather us together, and deliver us from the heathen, that we may give thanks to thy holy name, and glory in thy praise" (I Chronicles 16:29, 35).

LIVING IN GOD'S HOLY PRESENCE

The question is asked in Psalm 15:1, *"LORD, who shall dwell in thy tabernacle? who shall dwell in thy holy hill?"* The following verses answer these questions:

"He that walketh uprightly, and worketh righteousness, and speaketh the truth in his heart. He that backbiteth not with his tongue, nor doeth evil to his neighbour, nor taketh up a reproach against his neighbour. In whose eyes a vile person is contemned [despised]; but he honoureth them that fear the LORD. He that sweareth to his own hurt, and changeth not. He that putteth not out his money to usury, nor taketh reward against the innocent. He that doeth these things shall never be moved" (Psalm 15:2-5).

First, we must walk uprightly and righteously, which means that we must live above reproach. The life of Daniel would be a good example for us to follow.

"Then the presidents and princes sought to find occasion against Daniel concerning the kingdom; but they could find none occasion nor fault; forasmuch as he was faithful, neither was there any error or fault found in him. Then said these men, We shall not find any occasion against this Daniel, except we find it against him concerning the law of his God" (Daniel 6:4-5).

Daniel lived every day according to the Word of God. We cannot live one way on Sunday and then live differently during the other days of the week. To dwell in God's holy hill, we need to live uprightly in every area of our life, every day—whether it is being honest on our jobs, or honest when filing our tax returns. The Lord Jesus said, *"Render therefore unto Caesar the things which are Caesar's; and unto God the things that are God's"* (Matthew 22:21b).

Be honest in every part of your life, including the lending and borrowing of money between Christian brethren. *"He that hath not given forth upon usury, neither hath taken any increase, that hath withdrawn his hand from iniquity, hath executed true judgment between man and man"* (Ezekiel 18:8). (Read Ezekiel 18:1-9.) This verse is saying that Christians should not loan one another money with interest. The Lord Jesus said, *"and lend, hoping for nothing again"* (Luke 6:35b).

> *"But whoso hath this world's good, and seeth his brother have need, and shutteth up his bowels of compassion from him, how dwelleth the love of God in him? My little children, let us not love in word, neither in tongue; but in deed and in truth"* (I John 3:17-18).

Dr. Bob Jones, Sr., said, *It is never right to do wrong to get a chance to do right.* Working righteousness means that we do not justify spending our tithe money on gasoline so that we can drive to work or to church when finances are low. Nor do we use the Lord's Day for our own pleasure and entertainment. We take one day in seven to give wholly unto God, not because we are under the law, but to demonstrate our love to our Heavenly Father and to our Savior, Jesus Christ, by worshipping and reverencing their holiness. In order to walk uprightly and work righteousness we need to return to Biblical principles and follow them.

Walking uprightly also includes humility. Satan fell from Heaven because He became proud and thought to exalt himself above God Almighty.

"How art thou fallen from heaven, O Lucifer, son of the morning! how art thou cut down to the ground, which didst weaken the nations! For thou hast said in thine heart, I will ascend into heaven, I will exalt my throne above the stars of God: I will sit also upon the mount of the congregation, in the sides of the north" (Isaiah 14:12-13).

God is so holy that He had to condescend Himself in His own holy nature to look down upon man. *"The LORD looked down from heaven upon the children of men, to see if there were any that did understand, and seek God"* (Psalm 14:2). He didn't have to, but He did.

We need to reverence His holiness by humbling ourselves before Him. When the book of the law that God gave to Moses was read before King Josiah, he humbled himself before the Lord God Almighty.

"And it came to pass, when the king had heard the words of the law, that he rent his clothes. And the king commanded Hilkiah, and Ahikam the son of Shaphan, and Abdon the son of Micah, and Shaphan the scribe, and Asaiah a servant of the king's, saying, Go, enquire of the LORD for me, and for them that are left in Israel and in Judah, concerning the words of the book that is found: for great is the wrath of the LORD that is poured out upon us, because our fathers have not kept the word of the LORD, to do after all that is written in this book....And as for the king of Judah, who sent you to enquire of the LORD, so shall ye say unto him, Thus saith the LORD God of Israel concerning the words which thou hast heard; Because thine heart was tender, and thou

didst humble thyself before God, when thou heardest his words against this place, and against the inhabitants thereof, and humbledst thyself before me, and didst rend thy clothes, and weep before me; I have even heard thee also, saith the LORD" (II Chronicles 34:19-21, 26-27).

If we want to enter in the holy place of the Lord, we will have to humble ourselves before Him.

Second, we must speak the truth in our heart. Often times the things that are spoken and the belief of one's heart are contrary. The Lord Jesus said, *"Well hath Esaias prophesied of you hypocrites, as it is written, This people honoureth me with their lips, but their heart is far from me"* (Mark 7:6). The Lord knows whether or not we are speaking the truth, because He looks and sees our heart.

"But the LORD said unto Samuel, Look not on his countenance, or on the height of his stature; because I have refused him: for the LORD seeth not as man seeth; for man looketh on the outward appearance, but the LORD looketh on the heart" (I Samuel 16:7).

GOD DESPISES LYING

"Lying lips are abomination to the LORD: but they that deal truly are his delight" (Proverbs 12:22). If we want to draw close to the Lord in prayer and receive His blessings, then we need to speak the truth from our heart. Our Heavenly Father is interested in practical holiness; therefore, we need to live and walk holy before God by applying these practical Biblical commands.

Third, we must not be backbiters or do evil to our neighbor if we are going to approach the holy place of God in prayer. The sins that most often destroy our churches, our homes, our lives, and our walk with God are those that we cannot visibly detect in one another—things such as envy, strife, backbiting, gossip, and jealousy. *"Let us walk honestly, as in the day; not in rioting and drunkenness, not in chambering and wantonness, not in strife and envying. But put ye on the Lord Jesus Christ, and make not provision for the flesh, to fulfil the lusts thereof"* (Romans 13:13-14). *"For where envying and strife is, there is confusion and every evil work"* (James 3:16).

Those who *"backbiteth not with his tongue, nor doeth evil to his neighbor, nor taketh up a reproach against his neighbor"* will abide in God's holy place of prayer (Psalm 15:3).

Fourth, *"He that sweareth to his own hurt, and changeth not"* will abide in the holy place of God (Psalm 15:4). This means that we keep our word, regardless of consequences. We need to keep our word to family, friends, business associates, and everyone else—even if it cost us something. *"A good name is rather to be chosen than great riches, and loving favour rather than silver and gold"* (Proverbs 22:1).

God and His Son are holy; and every Christian was given the Holy Spirit of Christ on the day they got saved; therefore, we have access to the holy place where God dwells through His Holy Spirit. That access can be hindered when we grieve the Holy Spirit by our sinfulness. However, God is a reasonable God and full of mercy, so He has promised that if we confess our sins, He is faithful to forgive us and to cleanse us from all unrighteousness. *"If we confess our sins, he is faithful and just to forgive us our sins, and to cleanse us from all unrighteousness"* (I John 1:9).

Daily consider the condition of your heart before God and determine to live in His holy place of prayer. Keep your heart clean before God and follow after His commands so that you may enter into His holy place and pray.

Lesson Nine

The Priority of Prayer Questions
Part 2

1. What does the word *abide* mean?

_____

_____

2. Why is it that we cannot stand in God's presence in our human flesh and live?

_____

_____

3. What happened to Daniel and John when they saw a vision of God?

_____

_____

4. Why do seraphims cover their faces and feet when coming into the presence of God?

_____

_____

5.   What are the four things referenced in Psalm 24 that allow us to stand in God's holy place?

_____

_____

6.   According to Psalm 15, who shall dwell in God's holy hill?

_____

_____

7.   What does to live above reproach mean?

_____

_____

8.   Give an example of one way we can live above reproach.

_____

_____

9.   What does walking uprightly include?

_____

_____

10.   What does God have to do in order to look down upon man?

_____

_____

11.   Why is it important that we speak truth in our hearts?

_____

_____

_____

_____

_____

12. Name two sins that we cannot visibly detect but which can prevent us from approaching the holy place of God in prayer.

_____

_____

How Bad Do You Want It?

Introduction

"Now there was a certain man of Ramathaim-zophim, of mount Ephraim, and his name was Elkanah, the son of Jeroham, the son of Elihu, the son of Tohu, the son of Zuph, an Ephrathite: and he had two wives; the name of the one was Hannah, and the name of the other Peninnah: and Peninnah had children, but Hannah had no children. And this man went up out of his city yearly to worship and to sacrifice unto the LORD of hosts in Shiloh. And the two sons of Eli, Hophni and Phinehas, the priests of the LORD, were there. And when the time was that Elkanah offered, he gave to Peninnah his wife, and to all her sons and her daughters, portions: but unto Hannah he gave a worthy portion; for he loved Hannah: but the LORD had shut up her womb. And her adversary also provoked her sore, for to make her fret, because the LORD had shut up her womb. And as he did so year by year, when she went up to the house of the LORD, so she provoked her; therefore she wept, and did not eat. Then said Elkanah her husband to her, Hannah, why weepest thou? and why eatest thou not? and why is thy heart grieved? am not I better to thee than ten sons? So Hannah rose up after they had eaten in Shiloh, and after they had drunk. Now Eli the priest sat upon a seat by a post

of the temple of the LORD. *And she was in bitterness of soul, and prayed unto the* LORD, *and wept sore. And she vowed a vow, and said, O* LORD *of hosts, if thou wilt indeed look on the affliction of thine handmaid, and remember me, and not forget thine handmaid, but wilt give unto thine handmaid a man child, then I will give him unto the* LORD *all the days of his life, and there shall no razor come upon his head"* (1 Samuel 1:1-11).

HANNAH WAS SPECIFIC

Notice how specific Hannah was in her praying for a child; she specifically asked for a boy: *"And she vowed a vow, and said, O* LORD *of hosts...give unto thine handmaid a **man child"*** (I Samuel 1:11). Hannah longed desperately for a baby, specifically for a baby boy, and God answered her request.

We need to learn to be specific in our praying, whether it is praying for a spouse, a particular financial need, souls to be saved, or anything else that we are asking of our Heavenly Father. John Hyde, a missionary to India during the latter nineteenth and early twentieth centuries, was winning five souls a day to Christ at the end of his life because he was specifically asking God the Father for five souls a day.

HANNAH PERSISTED IN PRAYER

"And it came to pass, as she continued praying before the LORD, *that Eli marked her mouth. Now Hannah, she spake in her heart; only her lips moved, but her voice was not heard: therefore Eli thought she had been drunken. And Eli said unto her, How long wilt thou be drunken? put away thy wine from thee. And Hannah answered and said, No, my lord, I am a woman of a sorrowful spirit: I have drunk neither wine nor strong drink, but have poured out my soul before the* LORD. *Count not thine handmaid*

---

for a daughter of Belial: for out of the abundance of my complaint and grief have I spoken hitherto. Then Eli answered and said, Go in peace: and the God of Israel grant thee thy petition that thou hast asked of him" (I Samuel 1:12-17).

Many people say they want revival, they want their marriages to work, or they want something else. My question is, How badly do they want it? Hannah so desperately wanted a baby that she fasted, she wept, she grieved over it, and she continued to take her request before the Lord.

*"Then said Elkanah her husband to her, Hannah, why weepest thou? and why eatest thou not? and why is thy heart grieved? am not I better to thee than ten sons?...And...she **continued** praying before the LORD...."* (I Samuel 1:8, 12).

Hannah went to the temple year after year to pray and cry aloud unto God for a baby boy. She did not pray a day or two then give up, but she persisted and continued praying for a number of years. Like Hannah, if we want something badly enough, then we will not set any time limits on God; rather, we will keep going to Him with our petitions until He answers:

"For my thoughts are not your thoughts, neither are your ways my ways, saith the LORD. For as the heavens are higher than the earth, so are my ways higher than your ways, and my thoughts than your thoughts" (Isaiah 55:8-9).

When we go to God with a specific request, then we need to commit it to Him, continue praying for it, and leave it to God's timing. We do not know how many years Hannah continued praying, but we do know that it was years, because Peninnah had sons and daughters, and we know that each baby is usually carried in its mother's womb for nine months.

Many of us have not wanted something as badly as Hannah wanted a baby boy, because we have not persisted in prayer for our requests. A young lady that I know of said she wanted to have a baby, but after hearing the sermon I preached on Hannah's persistence, she said that if she had wanted a baby as badly as Hannah wanted one, she probably would have already had one. Three months after she began praying with the same urgency and persistence as Hannah, this young lady became with child and is now the mother of the long-desired baby.

How badly do we want souls to be saved? Do we really want those living on our street to be saved? If so, when was the last time you drove up and down your street praying that God would work in the hearts of your neighbors to be saved? How specifically are you praying for your neighborhood, your city, your state, your country? How persistently are you praying for them? Do you continue praying? Do you fast and weep over them? Do you ask God to provide opportunities for you to be a witness to them so that they will hear the Gospel of Jesus Christ? How long has it been since you went from business to business in your town and prayed in front of each business, asking God our Father to save the owners and the customers of those businesses? How long has it been since you took a Saturday evening and prayed over a map of your city, asking God to save souls and to deepen the walk of Christians that live there? How about praying for surrounding communities and the people that live in them? How persistently are you praying for the ministries at your church? The time to pray for them is not Sunday morning, but all during the week.

HANNAH PRAYED FERVENTLY

The Bible says, "The effectual fervent prayer of a righteous man availeth much"—James 5:16b. Our English word *fever* is derived from this word, *fervent*. When people have a fever, they are experiencing an increase in their normal body temperature, and it is a sign that something out of the ordinary is going on in their body. To pray with fervency is to pray with increased intensity that is out of the ordinary praying. Effectual prayer is the prayer that comes from the heart and produces or is able to produce a desired effect. Effectual praying is associated with weeping; Hannah *"wept sore"* (I Samuel 1:10). It takes water to grow a farmer's crop, and if we sincerely want something badly enough it will take our tears to move the heart of God. *"He that goeth forth and weepeth, bearing precious seed, shall doubtless come again with rejoicing, bringing his sheaves with him"* (Psalm 126:6).

Do you weep over your lost family to be saved? Do you weep over your city to turn to God? The churches in America, for the most part, are trying to grow a harvest of souls without weeping. Mothers used to spend hours at the altar, weeping for their children to be right with God. Men used to cry out to God to use their sons in the ministry. The apostle Paul and Moses are two examples of men in the Bible who effectually and fervently prayed for their nations to be saved. We need to pray with such compassion as they did, weeping over souls and their lost condition before God, and earnestly desiring for them to know the joy and peace of salvation.

HANNAH PRAYED BELIEVING

First of all, she came year after year after year. *"And as he did so year by year, when she went up to the house of the LORD, so she provoked her; therefore she wept, and did not eat"* (1 Samuel 1:7).

She put up with Penninah's provoking. Every year when they left home to go to Shiloh, Hannah knew what was coming. She knew that this woman was going to torment her, make fun of her prayers, make fun of her walk with God, make fun of her begging for a child that had not come.

I'm reminded of a conversation I had several years ago with one of the young ladies who was helping me take care of my invalid wife. (A total of eight ladies worked with us during the 28 years of my wife's illness.) This particular lady said, "Dr. Tom, I keep hearing all these stories about what God can do. I want to see Him do one of them."

I asked what she would like to see. She said she just noticed that the gas gauge showed we were almost empty, and we still had several hundred miles to drive. "I want to see God fill the tank like you talked about before."

I bowed my head and said, "Father, You know she wants to see You fill this gas tank, so You take care of that so You will be glorified." As we were coming upon a gas station, the Lord spoke to my heart and said, "Tom, pull into this station right here." I turned into the gas station, pulled up to the gas pump, and started filling the tank.

The devil said, "Hey, Tom, He didn't do it!"

I said, "Shut up, Satan; it's not full yet."

About the time the tank got full, the attendant came out of the station. He walked over to us and said, "Cowboy hat...certain car. Would you be a fella named Dr. Tom Williams?"

I said, "Yes, that's me."

He said, "A fella came by early this morning about 6 o'clock and said that a man would be stopping here, and that he would have on a cowboy hat and would be driving this kind of car" (indicating the car I was driving). "He told me he wanted me to fill up your tank." After the tank was full, the attendant used the money the guy gave him to pay for the gas and then gave me the change.

I do not know who that kind-hearted man was, and I did not know he was going to stop at that gas station. I just know where God told me to stop. The young lady was amazed. She said, "I will never question another thing you say, Preacher."

There is a God, and He is able; but we have to convince Him we need Him. He wants to be needed. Are you not glad when your children come to you and really have a need and they come to you for it and not somewhere else? I am so thrilled when my children come to me because they need a prayer answered and they ask me to help them pray about it. We have to let God know how badly we want something and let Him know that we believe He is our only source of help. God is able to answer our prayers; He just wants us to believe Him. He wants us to demonstrate our dependence upon Him by going to Him with our needs.

Hannah believed that God was her only source of help and hope; therefore, she didn't stop praying. When the answer to a prayer is delayed, many tend to stop praying because they have stopped believing. Notice that Hannah continued praying because she continued believing she was asking the only One who could grant her the desire of her heart.

LESSON TEN

HOW BAD DO YOU WANT IT?
QUESTIONS

1. Name someone who showed she wanted something very badly.

   _____

   _____

2. How was Hannah specific in her prayer?

   _____

   _____

3. After we go to God with our specific request, what is our next step?

   _____

   _____

4. What are some other things that Hannah did to show God how serious she was in this matter of prayer?

   _____

   _____

5. What is effectual prayer?

   _____

———

_____

_____

6. What is effectual prayer often associated with?

_____

_____

7. What are some things that we should be weeping over in our prayers?

_____

_____

8. What shows God that we believe He is our only source of help?

_____

_____

9. How can we demonstrate our dependency on Him?

_____

_____

10. What proved that Hannah truly believed God was her only source of help and that she believed Him?

_____

_____

———

ANSWER KEYS

LESSON ONE — HOW TO PRAY

1. Prayer isn't always answered immediately. Give an example from the Bible of someone who had to wait for their answer. **Daniel** (page 6)

2. Name 2 people in the Bible who had a prayer life. **Daniel and Jesus** (page 6)

3. In your own words, explain what "Pray about everything" means. **You pray for the smallest details to the greatest details in your life—from what to buy to who to marry.** (pages 6-7)

4. Find a verse that instructs us to pray. Write reference below. **Luke 18:1** (page 6)

5. Give examples of things in your everyday life that you can pray about. **Pastor, family, friends...** (page 7)

6. For what purpose was the Holy Spirit sent to us? **To teach us all things and bring all things to our remembrance that Jesus has said.** Give a verse to back up your answer. **John 14:26** (page 7)

7. Is there ever a time that we would ask Jesus for something? **No. We cast our cares on Jesus, but we do not ask Him for anything.** (page 7)

8. For what purpose do we pray to the Heavenly Father?
We make our petitions to Him. (page 5)

9. Why is it that you and I can call God "Father" but those in the Old Testament could not? **Christ had not come yet.** (page 8)

10. What does addressing God as our Father do?
Opens to us a greater depth of intimacy with Him (page 8)

LESSON 2 — THE PRIORITY OF PRAYER

1. How many times is prayer mentioned in the Bible?
More than 500 times (page 14)

2. What does God call the house of prayer? **His house** Give a verse to back up your answer. **Isaiah 56:7** (page 15)

3. What is the definition of the word *Christian*? **To be like Christ, or little Christ** (page 15)

4. What did Christ do before He did anything? **He prayed.** Give two references to back up your answer. **Matthew 14:23-31; Luke 6:12** (page 16)

5. Why is it important to pray before and after great acts of service? **To be continually armed for spiritual battle; so that the devil isn't given any ground to tempt us to be prideful; to renew and strengthen our mind and spirit** (page 16)

6. Why is it that Christians so often get "burned out" in the Christian life? **They are continuing in their own strength and not getting alone with God in prayer.** (page 16)

7. How does a person learn to pray? **By praying** (page 17)

8. What is the best way to come before God? **In secret.**
   Give two references in answer. **Matthew 6:6; Psalm 91:1**
   (page 17)

9. Give two examples of how we can show humility while praying. **Bowing your head; kneeling** (page 18)

10. What types of people does God often choose? **The weak, the
    foolish, the wicked, the harlots** (page 18)

11. What was the key factor in Daniel's prayer life? **He contin-
    ued in prayer.** (page 20)

12. Can we serve God without having a Bible? Explain your an-
    swer. **We can, because God made a way for us to commu-
    nicate with Him through prayer and the Holy Spirit who
    lives inside of us.** (page 20)

13. What will keep us from fainting (giving up) in our Christian
    life? **Prayer** (page 20)

14. If we are going to pray for others, what do we need to make
    sure of in our own life? **Make sure our hearts are clean be-
    fore God** (page 20)

LESSON THREE — THE WONDER OF PRAYER (PART 1)

1. How is it that we are able to come before God? **Through the
   Lord Jesus Christ** (page 25)

2. What does God allow us to ask in prayer? **Anything** (page 25)

3. What is one way that God will not answer our prayer? **If we
   ask amiss** (page 26)

4. How often does God want us to ask for something? **Continually** (page 26)

5. Give an example of someone in the Bible who continued to ask until God answered the prayer. **Abraham** (page 27)

6. Is there ever a time that you cannot go to God in prayer? **No** (page 27)

7. God answers the prayers of children. Give an example from the Bible where God heard the voice of a child. **Genesis 21:17-21** (page 28)

8. What characteristic does a child have that we should have when bowing in prayer? **Faith** (page 29)

9. Give an example of someone in the Bible who prayed for his city. **Jesus** (page 29)

10. State two things that Daniel did when praying for his nation. **Confessed his sin and made supplication** (page 29)

11. What is one thing that can move the heart of God when we earnestly pray? **Tears** (pages 29-30)

LESSON 4 — THE WONDER OF PRAYER (PART 2)

1. Give an example of someone in the Bible who prayed for an individual. **Moses prayed for Aaron.** (page 35)

2. How important is one soul? **More than all the wealth of the world.** Give a verse backing up your answer. **Matthew 16:26** (page 35)

3. What must we do if we are going to pray for someone? **Learn to love them for who they are** (page 36)

4. To what extent are we to love someone? **Like Christ loved us** (page 36)

5. Give a verse that shows us God loves us just the way we are. **Romans 5:8** (page 36)

6. What will help us begin to pray more? **Thinking on what God has done in answer to prayer** (page 37)

7. What is the most effective way to pray? **With fervency** (page 37)

8. What does the word "fervent" mean? **Zealous** (page 37)

9. How must we come to God in prayer in order to receive the promise of Him answering our prayer? **Believing** (page 37)

10. What does it show God when we continue to pray for something specifically? **That we believe Him** (page 39)

11. Give a verse stating that it is a sin to stop praying for someone. **1 Samuel 12:23** (page 40)

LESSON FIVE — THE WORK OF PRAYER

1. What does it mean to agonize in prayer? **To truly weep and even sweat from intensity.** (page 43)

2. How does the Bible describe the fervency and agony of our Savior's prayers in the Garden of Gethsemane? **Sweat drops of blood** (page 43)

3. What is the deepest thing you can want for your life? **God's will** (page 43)

4. What did Hannah do to show how serious she was about her request? **Fasted and wept** (pages 44)

5. How often did Hannah pray for a child? **Year by year** (page 44)

6. Who wrestled in prayer? **Jacob** (page 46)

7. What does it mean to wrestle in prayer? **Getting alone with God and not letting go until you receive an answer** (page 47)

8. Why is it important to be in prayer while soul-winning? **The Lord knows where to send you, and who will be ready to hear the Gospel message.** (page 49)

9. Give two examples from the Bible of someone getting saved. **Zacchaeus and the woman at the well** (pages 49-50)

10. Does everyone get saved the same way? Explain your answer. **No, because people receive things differently** (page 49)

11. Give the 5 steps you should take before you go out soul-winning. **1) Pray. 2) Cry over souls. 3) Plead for them from the heart. 4) Ask God for souls. 5) Expect God to answer and to give the increase.** (page 50)

LESSON SIX — THE HUMILITY OF PRAYER

1. Why is humility so important? **It declares our dependency upon God and heightens our awareness of God's ability and our inability to do anything apart from Him.** (page 53)

2. How does God respond to those that humble themselves?
He will lift them up. (page 53)

3. What are four things that Christians can do that will result in God healing our land? **Humble ourselves, pray, seek His face, and turn from our wicked ways** (page 53)

4. Who is the perfect example of humility?
Jesus Christ (pages 53-54)

5. How did Jesus' appearance portray humility?
He was common and ordinary-looking. (page 53)

6. How did Jesus' reputation portray humility? **He wasn't wealthy; He didn't have a house of His own; and even His clothing was made of the cheapest material.** (page 54)

7. Give two references that show Jesus being rejected by man.
Isaiah 53:3; John 1:11 (page 54)

8. What are two positions we can have to show humility when praying? **Bowing the head and kneeling** (pages 55-57)

9. What three positions in prayer are found in the Bible? **Standing with the head bowed, kneeling, or lying prostrate on one's face** (page 59)

10. Give three examples of people who kneeled while praying.
Solomon, Jesus, and Stephen (page 60-61)

LESSON SEVEN — HINDRANCES TO PRAYER

1. Is there ever a time God does not hear your prayers?
Yes, when we have unconfessed sin (page 65)

2. What should you do before you begin to pray? **Take time to examine your heart**. (page 65)

3. Give a verse showing how family relationships can affect prayers. **1 Peter 3:1** (page 65)

4. What does a wife need to do in her role in the family? **Be in subjection to her husband** (page 66)

5. What does a husband need to do in his role in the family? **Give honour to his wife** (page 66)

6. What is one thing a father might do toward his children that can hinder his prayers? **Incite his children to undue anger** (page 66)

7. What is iniquity? **Unrighteousness, sin, transgression, committing wrong against God** (page 67)

8. Where does sin start? **Sin starts in the heart.** (page 67)

9. How does a person become hardened toward God? **By disobedience** (page 68)

10. What happens when a person becomes hardened toward God? **When we call on God, He will not answer; and when we seek Him, we will not be able to find Him.** (page 69)

11. Give a verse stating if we become cold toward the poor, God will not hear our prayers. **Proverbs 21:13** (page 70)

12. How can we avoid becoming disobedient to God's commands? **By abiding in God's Word** (page 70)

13. How does a person remain teachable? **By keeping the heart and mind open to the Lord** (page 71)

14. What happens if we do not tell others about their sin? **Their blood will be on our hands, and our prayers can be hindered.** (page 72)

15. Give a verse showing that unbelief hinders prayers. **James 1: 6** (page 73)

16. How many times should you forgive someone? **70 times 7, meaning continually** (page 74)

LESSON EIGHT — THE HOLINESS OF PRAYER (PART 1)

1. By Whom can we become holy? **The Holy Spirit** (page 79)

2. How do we become holy? **By getting saved and then yielding to the Holy Spirit Who now lives in us** (page 79)

3. Why are we able to approach the Father in prayer? **Because of the holiness of His Son and His Spirit** (page 80)

4. What is holiness? **The absence of sin** (page 80)

5. Is it possible for God to sin? **No** (page 81)

6. What makes something holy? **God's presence** (page 81)

7. Give a Bible reference that shows us that God wants us to be holy. **1 Peter 1:15, 16** (page 82)

8. Give examples of people who did not let circumstances hinder them from following after God and holiness. **The three Hebrew children and Daniel** (page 82)

9. How do we perfect holiness? **By yielding to the Holy Spirit of Christ in us and not to the sinfulness of our flesh** (page 83)

10. Give a verse stating we can perfect holiness.
    II Corinthians 7:1 (page 83)

LESSON NINE — THE HOLINESS OF PRAYER (PART 2)

1. What does the word *abide* mean? **The word *abide* means "to live."** (page 87)

2. Why is it that we cannot stand in God's presence in our human flesh and live? **Because God is so holy and we are unholy** (page 87)

3. What happened to Daniel and John when they saw a vision of God? **John fell at the feet of God as though he were dead, and Daniel couldn't even stand.** (pages 87-88)

4. Why do seraphims cover their faces and feet when coming into the presence of God? **To reverence God's holiness** (page 88)

5. What are the four things referenced in Psalm 24 that allow us to stand in God's holy place? **Clean hands, pure heart, someone who has not lifted up his soul unto vanity nor sworn deceitfully** (page 88)

6. According to Psalm 15, who shall dwell in God's holy hill? **He that walketh uprightly, worketh righteousness, and speaketh the truth in his heart; he that backbiteth not with his tongue, nor doeth evil to his neighbor, nor taketh up a reproach against his neighbor** (page 88)

7. What does to live above reproach mean? **Walk uprightly and righteously** (page 89)

8. Give an example of one way we can live above reproach. **By being honest in our everyday life** (page 90)

9. What does walking uprightly include? **Humility** (page 91)

10. What does God have to do in order to look down upon man? **He has to condescend Himself in His own holy nature to look down upon man.** (page 91)

11. Why is it important that we speak truth in our hearts? **Because the Lord knows whether or not we are speaking the truth because He looks and sees our heart** (page 92)

12. Name two sins that we cannot visibly detect but which can prevent us from approaching the holy place of God in prayer. **Any of these: envy, strife, backbiting, gossip** (page 93)

LESSON 10 — HOW BAD DO YOU WANT IT?

1. Name someone who showed she wanted something very badly. **Hannah** (pages 97-98)

2. How was Hannah specific in her prayer? **She specifically asked for a boy.** (page 98)

3. After we go to God with our specific request, what is our next step? **To continually pray** (page 99)

4. What are some other things that Hannah did to show God how serious she was in this matter of prayer? **She fasted, wept, grieved, and continued bringing her request before the Lord.** (page 100)

5. What is effectual prayer? **The prayer that comes from the heart and produces or is able to produce a desired effect** (page 101)

6. What is effectual prayer often associated with? **Weeping** (page 101)

7. What are some things that we should be weeping over in our prayers? **Lost family to be saved, city to turn to God** (page 101)

8. What shows God that we believe He is our only source of help? **Continuing to pray and believe** (page 103)

9. How can we demonstrate our dependency on Him? **By going to Him with our needs** (page 03)

10. What proved that Hannah truly believed God was her only source of help and that she believed Him? **She didn't stop praying.** (page 103)